LABORATORY Manual

MATHEMATICS

CBSE Class XII

LABORATORY Manual

MATHEMATICS

CBSE Class XII

Authors

Rakesh Pandey, Sunil Rathore

Name..

Class........................ Section........................Roll No......................

School..

arihant
SUCCESS AND NOTHING LESS

Arihant Prakashan (School Division Series)

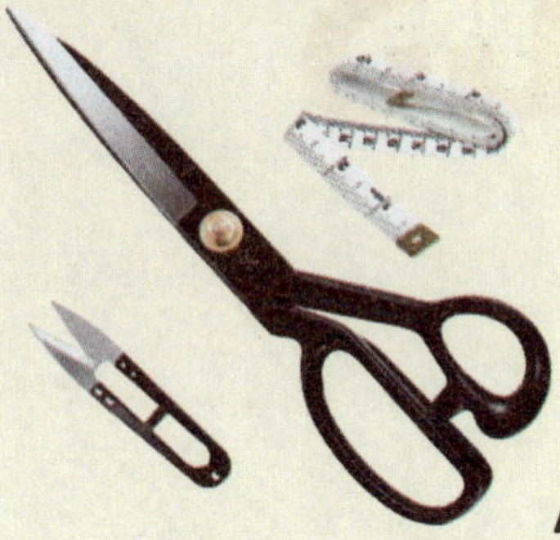
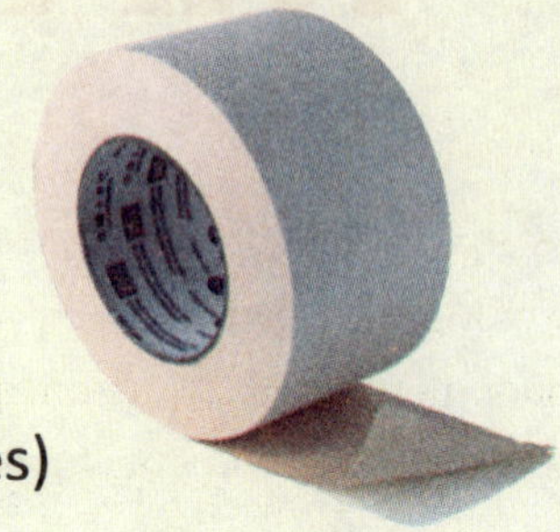

Arihant Prakashan (School Division Series)

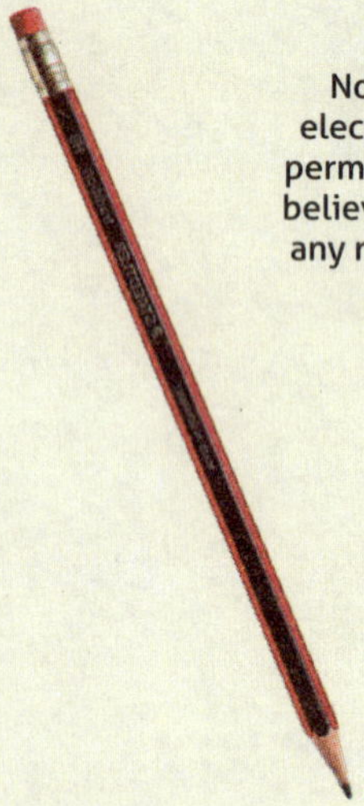

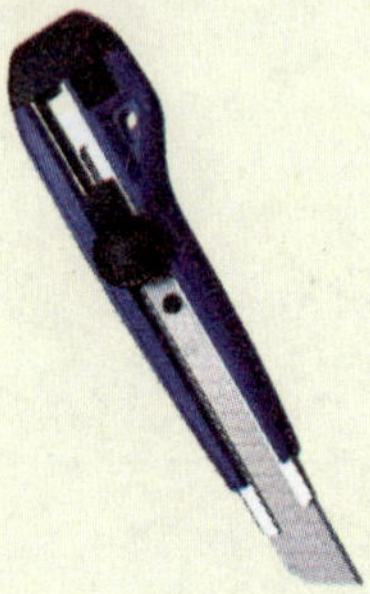

Administrative & Production Offices

Regd. Office

'Ramchhaya' 4577/15, Agarwal Road, Darya Ganj, New Delhi -110002
Tele: 011- 47630600, 43518550; Fax: 011- 23280316

Head Office

Kalindi, TP Nagar, Meerut (UP) - 250002, Tele: 0121-7156203, 7156204

Sales & Support Offices

Agra, Ahmedabad, Bengaluru, Bareilly, Chennai, Delhi, Guwahati, Hyderabad, Jaipur, Jhansi, Kolkata, Lucknow, Nagpur & Pune

Price : ₹ 350.00

PO No. : TXT-59-T071648-6-26

Published by Arihant Publications (India) Ltd.

For further information about the books from Arihant, log on to **www.arihantbooks.com** or email to **info@arihantbooks.com**

Follow us on

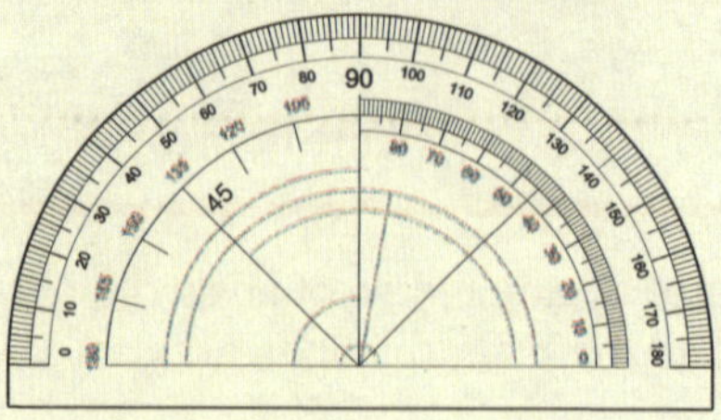

Contents

ACTIVITIES

PROJECTS

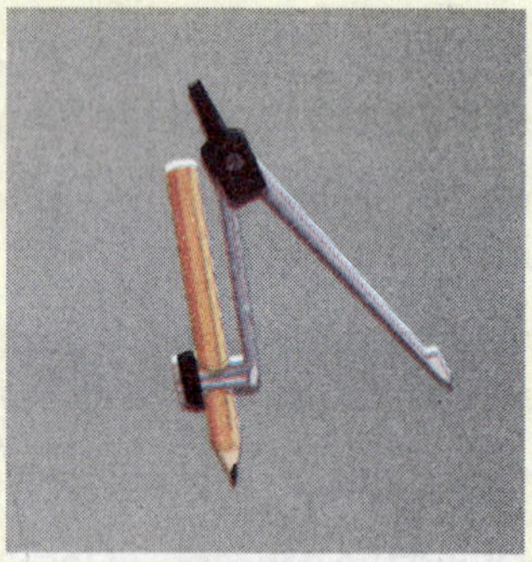

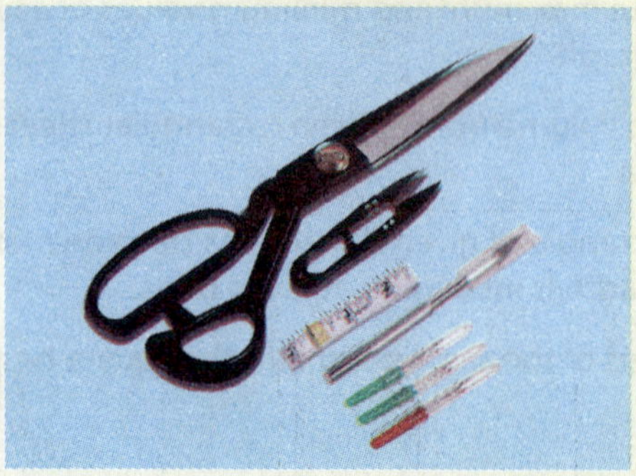

Set-up of Mathematics Laboratory

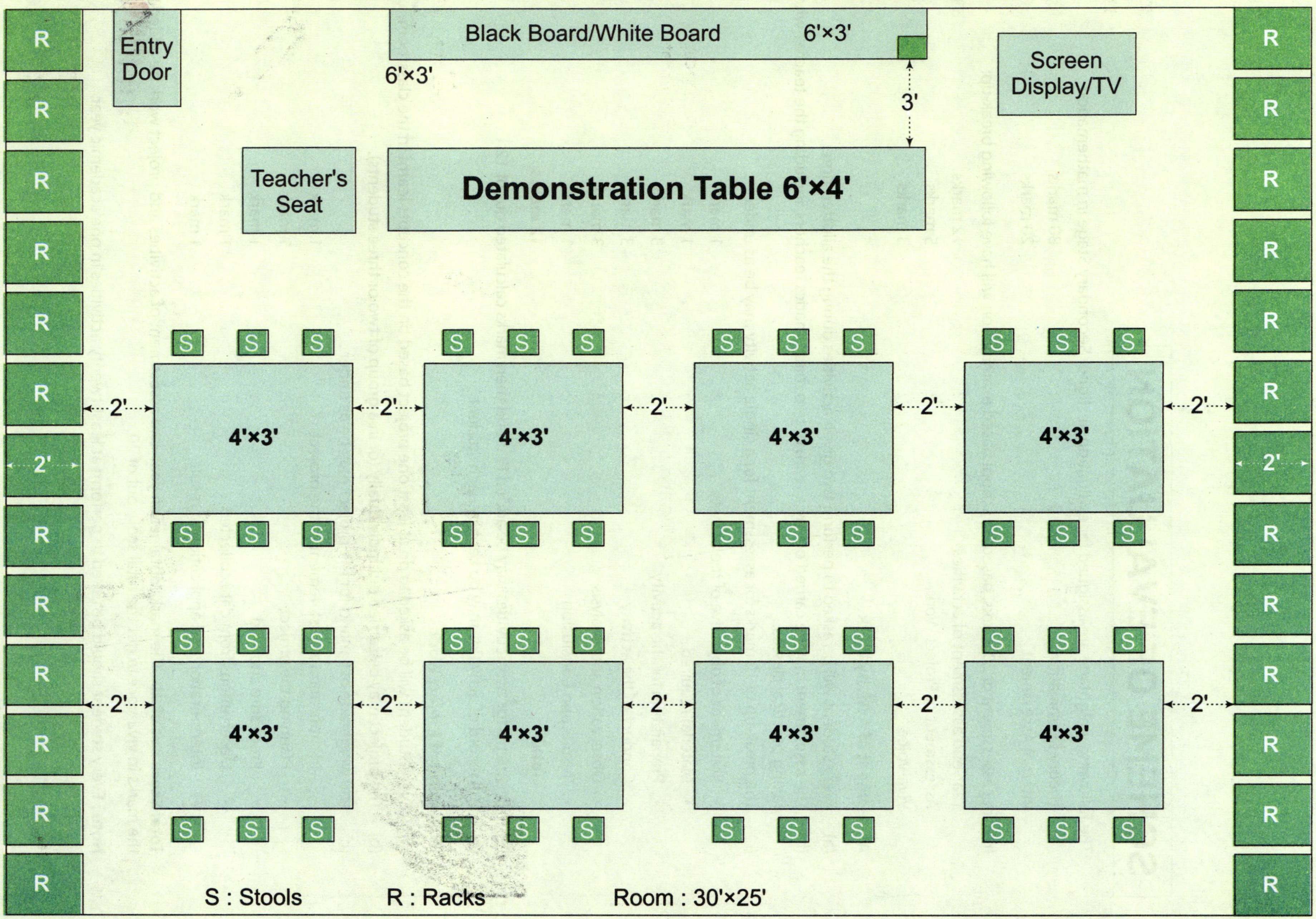

SCHEME OF EVALUATION

The following weightage are assigned for evaluation at Higher Secondary Stage in mathematics:

Theory Examination	:	80 marks
Internal Assessment	:	20 marks

Internal assessment of 20 marks, based on school based examination will have following break-up:

Year-end assessment of activities	:	12 marks
Assessment of Project Work	:	5 marks
Viva-voice	:	3 marks

Assessment of Activity Work

(a) Every student will be asked to perform two given activities during the allotted time.

(b) The assessment may be carried out by a team of two mathematics teachers, including the teacher who is taking practical classes.

(c) The break-up of 12 marks for assessment for a single activity may be as under:

• Statement of objective of the activity	:	1 mark
• Material required	:	1 mark
• Preparation for the activity	:	3 marks
• Conduct of the activity	:	3 marks
• Observation and analysis	:	3 marks
• Results and Conclusion	:	1 mark
Total	**:**	**12 marks**

(d) The marks for two activities may be added first and then marks calculated out of 12.

(e) Full record of activities may be kept by each student.

Evaluation of Project Work

(a) Every student will be asked to do at least one project based on the concepts learnt in the classroom.

(b) The project may be carried out individually (or in a group of two or three students).

(c) The weightage of 5 marks for the project may be as under :

• Identification and statement of the project	:	1 mark
• Planning the project	:	1 mark
• Procedure adopted	:	1 mark
• Observations from data collected	:	1 mark
• Interpretation and application of result	:	1 mark

Total Score out of 20 : The marks obtained in year-end assessment of activities and project work be added to the marks in viva-voce to get the total score out of 20.

Note : Every student should be asked to perform at least twenty activities in one academic year.

INDEX

S.No.	Name of the Activity/Project	Page No.	Date	Remarks

INDEX

S.No.	Name of the Activity/Project	Page No.	Date	Remarks

INDEX

S.No.	Name of the Activity/Project	Page No.	Date	Remarks

INDEX

S.No.	Name of the Activity/Project	Page No.	Date	Remarks

INDEX

S.No.	Name of the Activity/Project	Page No.	Date	Remarks

INDEX

S.No.	Name of the Activity/Project	Page No.	Date	Remarks

LABORATORY Manual

MATHEMATICS

CERTIFICATE

This is to certify that Activities &
Projects recorded in this Practical Notebook
have been performed by ______________________
(Student's name)
of __________ of ______________________________
(class/section) (school name)
during academic session ______________________

....	....	....
Examiner Signature	Principal Signature (with school stamp)	Teacher Signature

MATERIALS AND EQUIPMENTS FOR MATHEMATICS LABORATORY

Following is the list of suggested instruments/models for the laboratory:

EQUIPMENT

Mathematical instrument set (Wooden Geometry Box for demonstration containing rulers, set-squares, divider, protractor and compasses),
some geometry boxes, metre scales of 100 cm, 50 cm and 30 cm, measuring tape, diagonal scale, clinometer, calculators, computers including related software etc.

MODELS FOR DEMONSTRATION OF

- Sets
- Relations and Functions
- Sine and cosine functions
- Quadratic functions with the help of linear functions
- Complex numbers
- Sequences and series
- Pascal's triangle
- Arithmetic Progressions
- Circles
- Conic Sections
- Limits and Derivatives
- Inequalities
- Exponential and logarithmic functions
- Increasing and decreasing functions
- Maxima, minima and point of inflection
- Angle in semicircle using vectors
- Construction of parabola when distance between directrix and focus is given
- Construction of ellipse when major and minor axes are given
- Octants (In three dimensional space)
- Shortest distance between two skew lines
- Geometrical interpretation of scalar and vector product
- Equation of a straight line passing through a fixed point and parallel to a given vector
- Projection of the line segment
- Sample spaces
- Conditional Probability

The Purpose of The Mathematics Laboratory

The main objective of mathematics is to train the students to think and analysis the given situations and act logically. These objectives can only be achieved if there is an opportunity of creating a scope of exploring, verifying and experimenting upon mathematical results by students themselves.

Since, activities create interest among students who wants to explore, and test some of their ideas, beliefs about mathematics and also present a problem or a challenge with the possibility of generating futher challenges and problems. Thus, there is need of adopting activity — oriented process rather than merely concentrating upon mastery of rules and formulae so as to pass out the examinations.

Mathematics laboratory is a place where scientific research and experiments are conducted for verification, exploration or discovery. The role of laboratory is helpful in understanding the mathematical concepts, formulae through activities.

A mathematics laboratory can foster mathematical awareness, skill building, positive attitude and learning by doing experiments in various topics of mathematics such as Algebra, Geometry, Mensuration, Trigonometry, Calculus, Coordinate Geometry, etc. It is the place where students can generate problem and struggle to answer and learn certain concepts using concrete objects and verify many mathematical facts and properties using models, measurements and other activities.

The laboratory will act as a forum for the teachers to discuss and deliberate on some important mathematical issues.

Mathematics laboratory is expected to offer the following opportunities to learners:

- To discover the pattern for getting insight into the formulae
- To visualise algebraic and analytical results geometrically.
- Offers more scope for individual participation. It encourages students to become independent learners.
- To encourage students in recognising, extending, formulating patterns and enabling them to pose problems in the form of conjectures.
- To perform certain recreational activities in mathematics.
- To exhibit relatedness of mathematics with day to day life problems.
- Builds up inherent interest and confidence in the students towards learning and doing mathematics.
- It helps to supplement the knowledge learned in classroom.

Role of Mathematics Laboratory in Teaching-Learning

Mathematics at Senior Secondary stage is a little more abstract as compared to the subject at the secondary stage. The mathematics laboratory at this stage can contribute in a big way to the learning of this subject. Some of the ways are:

- Here the student will get an opportunity to understand the abstract ideas/ concepts through concrete objects and situations.
- The concepts of relations and functions can be easily understood by making working models and by making arrow diagrams using wires.
- Three dimensional concepts can only be conceived by three dimensional models in the laboratory, where as it is very difficult to understand these concepts on a black board.
- The concept of function and its inverse function, becomes very clear by drawing their graphs using mathematical instruments and using the concept of image about the line y=x, which can be done only in the laboratory.
- Since, the larger time available individually to the student and opportunity to repeat an activity several times, students can revise and rethink the problem and solutions. It helps to develop metacognitive abilities.
- It widens the experiential base and lays groundwork for later learning of new areas of mathematics and helps to make approprite connection between the known and unknown in mathematics.

Management and Maintenance of Laboratory

A laboratory is equipped with instruments, apparatus, equipments, models apart from facilities like water, electricity, etc. Non-availability of a single material or facility out of these may hinder the performance of any experiment activity in the laboratory. Therefore, the laboratory must be well managed and well maintained.

Personal Management and Maintenance

In personal management and maintenance following points are considered:

1. **Cleanliness** A laboratory should always be neat and clean. When students perform experiment activities during the day, it certainly becomes dirty and things are scattered. So, it is the duty of the lab staff to clean the laboratory.
2. **Checking and arranging materials for the day's work** Lab staff should know that what activities are going to be performed on a particular day. The material required for the day's activities must be arranged one day before.
3. The facilities like water, electricity, etc. must be checked and made available at the time of experiments.
4. Identify the necessary materials required in the laboratory by labeling them with name tags.
5. Many safety measures are required while working in laboratory. A list of such measures may be pasted on a wall of the laboratory.
6. Electrification of the laboratory should be professionally done to allow for safety use.
7. A first aid kit may be kept in the laboratory.

Management and Maintenance of Materials

To manage and maintain materials for a laboratory following points must be considered:

1. A list of instruments, apparatus, activities and material may be prepared according to the experiments included in the syllabus of mathematics.
2. Arrange the materials in places (on tables, shelves, board, etc) in a way that they can be easily accessed when needed and returned appropriately after use.
3. The instruments, equipments and apparatus should also be checked regularly by the laboratory staff. If any repair is required it should be done immediately.
4. Arrange the benches and tables to allow for free movement in the laboratory.

Materials and Equipments for Mathematics Laboratory

As the students will be involved in a lot of model making activities under the guidance of the teacher, the smooth running of the mathematics laboratory will depend upon the supply of oddments such as strings and threads, cellotape, white cardboard, hardboard, needles and pins, drawing pins, sandpaper, pliers, screwdrivers, rubber bands of different colours, gummed papers and labels, squared papers, plywood, scissors, saw, paint, soldering, solder wire, steel wire, cotton wool, tin and plastic sheets, glazed papers, overhead projector, slide projector, epidiascope, liquid crystal display etc.

Besides these, some models, charts, slides, etc., made up of a good durable material should also be there for the teacher to demonstrate some mathematical concepts, facts and properties before the students. Different tables, ready reckner should also be there (in the laminated form) so that these can be used by the students for different purposes.

In view of the above, following is the list of suggested instruments/models for the laboratory:

Equipment

Mathematical instrument set (Wooden Geometry Box for demonstration containing rulers, set-squares, divider, protractor and compasses), some geometry boxes, metre scales of 100 cm, 50 cm and 30 cm, measuring tape, diagonal scale, clinometer, calculators, computers including related software etc.

Models

For demonstration of

- Sets
- Relations and Functions
- Sine and cosine functions
- Quadratic functions with the help of linear functions
- Complex number
- Principle of mathematical induction
- Sequence and series
- Pascal's triangle
- Arithmetic Progression
- Circle
- Conic Sections
- Limits and Derivatives
- Inequality

- Exponential and logarithmic functions
- Increasing, decreasing functions
- Maxima, minima, point of inflection
- Lagrange's minima, point of inflection
- Rolle's theorem
- Definite Integral as limit of sum
- Angle in semicircle using vectors
- Construction of parabola when distance between directrix and focus is given
- Construction of ellipse when major and minor axes are given
- Octants (In three dimensional space)
- Shortest distance between two skew lines
- Geometrical interpretation of scalar and vector product
- Equation of a straight line passing through a fixed point and parallel to a given vector
- Equation to a plane
- Angle between two planes
- Bisection of the angles between two planes by a third plane
- Intersection of three planes
- Projection of the line segment
- Sample spaces
- Conditional Probability

Activities

Activity 1

OBJECTIVE

To verify that the relation R in the set L of all lines in a plane, defined by $R = \{(l, m) : l \perp m\}$ is symmetric but neither reflexive nor transitive.

Material Required

A piece of cardboard, 8 pieces of wires, some nails, white paper, gum etc.

Prerequisite Knowledge

1. Concept of relation.
2. Concept of types of relation (reflexive, symmetric and transitive).

Method of Construction

Take a piece of cardboard and paste a white paper on it. Fix all the 8 wires randomly on the cardboard with the help of nails such that some of them are parallel, some are perpendicular to each other and some are inclined at some angle as shown in the figure given below.

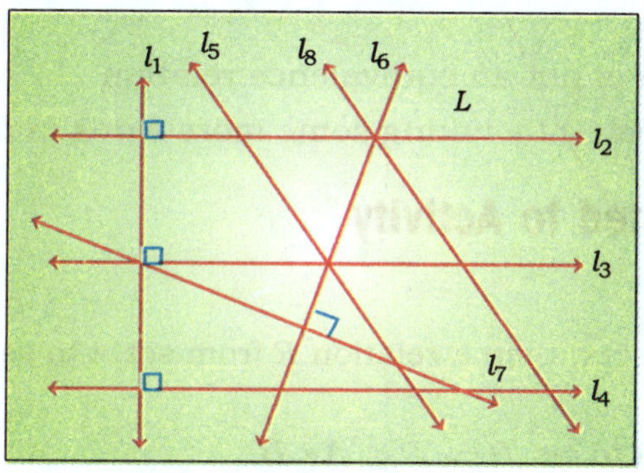

Fig. 1.1

Demonstration

1. Let the wires represent the lines $l_1, l_2, ..., l_8$.
2. l_1 is perpendicular to each of the lines l_2, l_3, l_4 [see above figure].
3. l_6 is perpendicular to l_7.
4. l_2 is parallel to l_3, l_3 is parallel to l_4 and l_5 is parallel to l_8.
5. $(l_1, l_2), (l_1, l_3), (l_1, l_4), (l_6, l_7) \in R$

Observation

1. In the Figure (1.1), no line is perpendicular to itself, so the relation $R = \{(l, m) : l \perp m\}$ ...... reflexive. (is/is not)
2. In Figure (1.1), $l_1 \perp l_2$. Is $l_2 \perp l_1$? .... (Yes/No)

   $\therefore (l_1, l_2) \in R \Rightarrow (l_2, l_1)$........... $R(\notin / \in)$

   Similarly, $l_3 \perp l_1$. Is $l_1 \perp l_3$? .... (Yes/No)

   $\therefore (l_3, l_1) \in R \Rightarrow (l_1, l_3)$........... $R(\notin / \in)$

   Also, $l_6 \perp l_7$. Is $l_7 \perp l_6$? .... (Yes/No)

   $\therefore (l_6, l_7) \in R \Rightarrow (l_7, l_6)$........... $R(\notin / \in)$

   $\therefore$ The relation R .... symmetric. (is/is not)
3. In Figure (1.1), $l_2 \perp l_1$ and $l_1 \perp l_3$. Is $l_2 \perp l_3$? .... (Yes/No)

   i.e. $(l_2, l_1) \in R$ and $(l_1, l_3) \in R$

   $\Rightarrow (l_2, l_3)$........ $R(\notin / \in)$

   $\therefore$ The relation R .... transitive. (is/is not)

Result

The given relation is symmetric but neither reflexive nor transitive.

Application

On the basis of this activity, we can check whether a given relation is an equivalence relation or not.

Note

1. In this case, the relation is not an equivalence relation.
2. This activity can be repeated by taking some more wires in different positions.

Necessary Concepts Related to Activity

1. Relation

Let A and B be two non-empty sets, then a relation R from set A to set B is a subset of the cartesian product of set A with set B.

Thus, R is a relation from set A to set $B \Leftrightarrow R \subseteq A \times B$.

2. Types of Relation

(i) **Reflexive relation** A relation R on a set A is said to be reflexive if every element of set A is related to itself. Thus, R is reflexive $\Leftrightarrow (a, a) \in R$ i.e. $aRa \; \forall a \in A$.

(ii) **Symmetric relation** A relation R on a set A is said to be a symmetric relation iff,

$(a, b) \in R \Rightarrow (b, a) \in R \; \forall \; a, b \in A$.

i.e. $aRb \Rightarrow bRa \; \forall \; a, b \in A$

(iii) **Transitive relation** A relation R on a set A is said to be a transitive relation, iff

$(a, b) \in R$ and $(b, c) \in R \Rightarrow (a, c) \in R \; \forall \; a, b, c \in A$.

i.e. aRb and $bRc \Rightarrow aRc \; \forall \; a, b, c \in R$

Viva-Voce

Q.1 Define a relation.

Ans Let A and B be two sets, then a relation R from set A to set B is a subset of $A \times B$.
Thus, R is a relation from set A to set $B \Leftrightarrow R \subseteq A \times B$.

Q.2 What is the necessary condition for a relation to be reflexive?

Ans A relation R on a set A is said to be reflexive if every element of A is related to itself.
Thus, R is reflexive $\Leftrightarrow (a, a) \in R \ \forall \ a \in A$

Q.3 Write the smallest reflexive relation on set $A = \{1, 2, 3\}$

Ans $\{(1, 1), (2, 2), (3, 3)\}$

Q.4 State the reason for the relation R on the set $A = \{1, 2, 3\}$ given by $R = \{(1, 2), (2, 1)\}$ not to be transitive.

Ans We observe that $(1, 2) \in R$ and $(2, 1) \in R$ but $(1, 1) \notin R$. Hence, R is not transitive.

Q.5 A relation 'is not equal to' is defined on R, it is reflexive, symmetric and transitive?

Ans The relation is symmetric only.

Q.6 Define a symmetric relation.

Ans A relation R on a set A is said to be a symmetric relation iff

$$(a, b) \in R \Rightarrow (b, a) \in R \ \forall \ a, b \in A$$

Q.7 Define a transitive relation.

Ans Let A be any set. A relation R on set A is said to be a transitive relation iff

$$(a, b) \in R \text{ and } (b, c) \in R \Rightarrow (a, c) \in R \ \forall \ a, b, c \in A$$

Q.8 Let $A = \{0, 1, 2, 3\}$ and R be a relation on set A defined as

$$R = \{(0, 0), (0, 1), (0, 3), (1, 0), (1, 1), (2, 2), (3, 0), (3, 3)\}$$

Is R reflexive? Symmetric ? Transitive ?

Ans R is reflexive and symmetric but not transitive.

Activity 2

OBJECTIVE

To verify that the relation R in the set L of all lines in a plane, defined by $R = \{(l, m) : l \parallel m\}$ is an equivalence relation.

Material Required

A piece of cardboard, 8 pieces of wire, some nails, white paper, gum etc.

Prerequisite Knowledge

1. Concept of relation and its types.
2. Equivalence relation.

Method of Construction

Take a piece of cardboard and paste a white paper on it. Fix all the 8 wires randomly on the cardboard with the help of nails such that some of them are parallel, some are perpendicular to each other and some are inclined as shown in the figure given below.

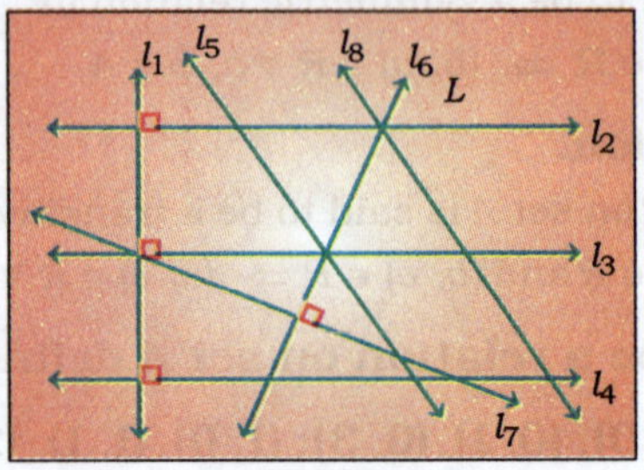

Fig. 2.1

Demonstration

1. Let the wires represent the lines $l_1, l_2, ..., l_8$.
2. l_1 is perpendicular to each of the lines l_2, l_3, l_4 [see above figure].
3. l_6 is perpendicular to l_7.
4. l_2 is parallel to l_3, l_3 is parallel to l_4 and l_5 is parallel to l_8.
5. $(l_2, l_3), (l_3, l_4), (l_5, l_8) \in R$

Observation

1. In Figure (2.1), every line is parallel to itself. So, the relation $R = \{(l, m) : l \| m\}$ ....reflexive relation. (is/is not)
2. In Figure (2.1), observe that $l_2 \| l_3$. Is $l_3 \| l_2$? .... (Yes/No)

   So, $(l_2, l_3) \in R \Rightarrow (l_3, l_2) .... R (\notin / \in)$
   Similarly, $l_3 \| l_4$. Is $l_4 \| l_3$? .... (Yes/No)
   So, $(l_3, l_4) \in R \Rightarrow (l_4, l_3) .... R (\notin / \in)$
   and $(l_5, l_8) \in R \Rightarrow (l_8, l_5) .... R (\notin / \in)$
   $\therefore$ The relation R .... symmetric relation. (is / is not)

3. In Figure (2.1), observe that $l_2 || l_3$ and $l_3 || l_4$. Is $l_2 || l_4$? .... (Yes/No)

So, $(l_2, l_3) \in R$ and $(l_3, l_4) \in R \Rightarrow (l_2, l_4) .... R (\notin / \in)$

Similarly, $l_3 || l_4$ and $l_4 || l_2$. Is $l_3 || l_2$? .... (Yes/No)

So, $(l_3, l_4) \in R$, $(l_4, l_2) \in R \Rightarrow (l_3, l_2) .... R (\notin / \in)$

Thus, the relation R .... transitive relation. (is / is not)

Hence, the relation R is reflexive, symmetric and transitive. So, R is an equivalence relation.

Result

The given relation is an equivalence relation.

Application

From this activity, we can easily understand the concept of an equivalence relation.

Note *This activity can be repeated by fixing some more wires in different positions.*

Necessary Concepts Related to Activity

1. **Relation** Refer to activity 1.
2. **Equivalence relation** A relation R on a set A is said to be an equivalence relation iff, it is
   (i) **Reflexive** Refer to Activity 1. (ii) **Symmetric** Refer to Activity 1.
   (iii) **Transitive** Refer to Activity 1.

Viva-Voce

Q.1 Define an equivalence relation.

Ans A relation R on a set A is said to be an equivalence relation if it is reflexive, symmetric and transitive.

Q.2 Give a practical example of an equivalence relation.

Ans R be a relation on the set B of all books in a library, defined by

$R = \{(a, b) : a$ and b have equal number of pages$\}$.

Q.3 The union of two equivalence relations on a set is not necessarily an equivalence relation. Is True or False?

Ans True. Let $A = \{a, b, c\}$ and R and S be two relations on A, given by

$R = \{(a, a), (b, b), (c, c), (a, b), (b, a)\}$ and

$S = \{(a, a), (b, b), (c, c), (b, c), (c, b)\}$

Both R and S are equivalence relations. But $R \cup S$ is not transitive, because $(a, b) \in R \cup S$ and $(b, c) \in R \cup S$ but $(a, c) \notin R \cup S$.

Q.4 Write the smallest equivalence relation on the set $A = \{1, 2, 3\}$

Ans $\{(1, 1), (2, 2), (3, 3)\}$

Q.5 For the set $A = \{1, 2, 3\}$ a relation R on the set A is defined as follows

$$R = \{(1, 1), (2, 2), (3, 3), (1, 3)\}$$

Write the ordered pairs to be added to R to make the smallest equivalence relation.

Ans (3, 1)

Q.6 The intersection of two equivalence relations on a non-empty set A is an equivalence relation. True or False?

Ans True

Q.7 From $aR_1b \Leftrightarrow |a| = |b|$, $aR_2b \Leftrightarrow a$ divides b, $aR_3b \Leftrightarrow a < b$. Which is an equivalence relation?

Ans Only $aR_1b \Leftrightarrow |a| = |b|$ is an equivalence relation.

Q.8 Is it true, the inverse of an equivalence relation is an equivalence relation?

Ans Yes.

Q.9 It is true every relation which is symmetric and transitive is also reflexive?

Ans No.

Activity 3

OBJECTIVE

To demonstrate a function which is not one-one but is onto.

Material Required

A piece of cardboard, some nails, some strings of 5-6 cm length, gum and some plastic strips.

Prerequisite Knowledge

1. Concept of function.
2. Concept of one-one function.
3. Concept of onto function.

Method of Construction

1. Paste a plastic strip on the left hand side of the cardboard and fix three nails on it as shown in the Figure 3.1 (a). Name them as 1, 2 and 3.
2. Paste another strip on the right hand side of the cardboard and fix two nails in the plastic strip as shown in Figure 3.1 (b). Name them as *a* and *b*.
3. Join the nails on the left strip to the nails on the right strip as shown in Figure 3.1 (c).

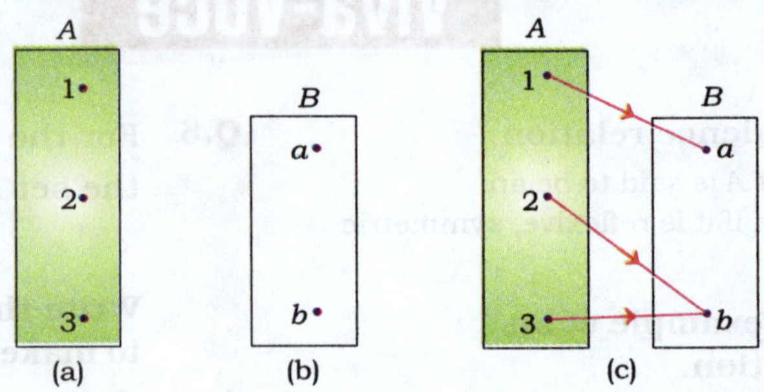

Fig. 3.1

Demonstration

1. Take the set $A = \{1, 2, 3\}$
2. Take the set $B = \{a, b\}$
3. Join elements of set A to the elements of set B as shown in Figure 3.1 (c).

Observation

1. The image of the element 1 of A in B is ....

   The image of the element 2 of A in B is ....

   The image of the element 3 of A in B is ....

   So, Figure 3.1 (c) represents a ......
2. Every element in A has a image in B.

   So, the function is ...... (one-one/not one-one).
3. The pre-image of each element of B in A .... (exists / does not exist). So, the function is .... (onto/ not onto).

Result

The function is not one-one but is onto.

Application

This activity is very helpful to understand the concept of one-one and onto functions.

Note *Demonstrate the same activity by increasing the number of the elements (nails) of sets A and B.*

Necessary Concepts Related to Activity

1. Function

Let A and B be two non-empty sets. A function from set A to set B is a relation from A to B (denoted by f) satisfying the following conditions

(i) for each $a \in A$, there exists $b \in B$ such that $(a, b) \in f$.

(ii) no two distinct ordered pairs in f have the same first element.

If f is a function from set A to set B and $(a, b) \in f$, then we can write $f(a) = b$, where b is called the **image** of a under f and a is called the **pre-image** of b under f.

2. One-One Function

A function $f: A \to B$ is said to be a one-one function or an **injective function** if distinct elements of A have distinct images in B.

Thus, $f: A \to B$ is one-one, if $a \neq b$, then $f(a) \neq f(b)$ and if $f(a) = f(b)$, then $a = b \; \forall \; a, b \in A$.

3. Onto Function

A function $f: A \to B$ is said to be an onto function, if every element of B is the f-image of some element of A, i.e. $f(a) = b$ or range of f is the co-domain of f.

Thus, $f: A \to B$ is onto iff for each $b \in B$, there exists $a \in A$ such that $f(a) = b$.

It is also known as **surjective function**.

Viva-Voce

Q.1 Write the condition for a function $f: x \to y$ to be one-one.

Ans A function $f: x \to y$ is said to be one-one, if for every $x_1, x_2 \in x$, $f(x_1) = f(x_2) \Rightarrow x_1 = x_2$

Q.2 What do you mean by injective function?

Ans A function $f: A \to B$ is said to be a one-one function or an injective function if distinct elements of A have distinct images in B.

Q.3 Let A be the set of all 50 students of class XII in a school. Let $f: A \to N$ be a function defined by $f(x)$ = Roll number of student x. State whether it is one-one or not.

Ans Since, no two different students of the class can have the same roll number. Therefore, f is one-one.

Q.4 Is cos x one-one or not?

Ans We know that, $\cos 0 = \cos 2\pi = 1$.

Hence, $\cos x$ is not one-one

Q.5 Let $A = \{-1, 0, 1\}$ and $f(x) = x^2$, $x \in A$. Find whether $f(x)$ is one-one or not.

Ans We have, $f(-1) = (-1)^2 = 1$ and $f(1) = (1)^2 = 1$

$\therefore \; f(-1) = f(1)$

But $-1 \neq 1$

Hence, $f(x)$ is not one-one.

Activity 4

OBJECTIVE

To demonstrate a function which is one-one but not onto.

Material Required

A piece of cardboard, some nails, some strings of 5-6 cm length, gum and some plastic strips.

Prerequisite Knowledge

1. Concept of function. 2. Concept of one-one function. 3. Concept of onto function.

Method of Construction

1. Paste a plastic strip on the left hand side of the cardboard and fix two nails on it as shown in Figure 4.1 (a). Name them as a and b.
2. Paste another strip on the right hand side of the cardboard and fix three nails on it as shown in Figure 4.1 (b). Name them as 1, 2 and 3.
3. Join the nails on the left strip to the nails on the right strip as shown in the Figure 4.1 (c).

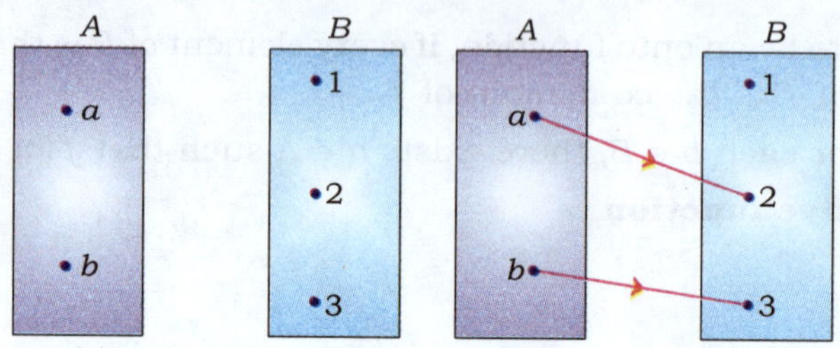

(a) (b) (c)

Fig. 4.1

Demonstration

1. Take the set $A = \{a, b\}$.
2. Take the set $B = \{1, 2, 3\}$.
3. Join elements of set A to the elements of set B as shown in Figure 4.1 (c).

Observation

1. The image of the element a of set A in set B is ....

   The image of the element b of set A in set B is ....

   So, the Figure 4.1 (c) represents a ....
2. Every element in set A has a unique image in set B. So, the function is .... (one-one/not one-one).
3. The pre-image of the element 1 of set B in set A .... (exists / does not exist). So, the function is .... (onto/ not onto).

   Thus, Figure 4.1 (c) represents a function which is .... but not onto.

Result

The function is one-one but not onto.

Application

This activity is very useful to understand the concept of one-one and onto functions.

Note *Demonstrate the same activity by increasing the number of the elements (nails) of set A and B .*

Necessary Concepts Related to Activity

1. **Function** Refer to Activity 3.
2. **One-one function** Refer to Activity 3.
3. **Onto function** Refer to Activity 3.

Viva-Voce

Q.1 Define onto function.

Ans A function $f : A \rightarrow B$ is said to be an onto function if every element of B is the f-image of some element of A.

Q.2 Give another name of onto function.

Ans Onto function is also known as a surjective function.

Q.3 Give condition for a function to be bijective.

Ans For a function to be bijective it must be injective (one-one) and surjective (onto) both.

Q.4 For a function $f(x) = \sin x$ on R to be onto, what must be its codomain.

Ans For a function to be onto, codomain must be equal to range of the function

$\therefore$ For $f(x) = \sin x$ to be onto

Codomain = Range of $\sin x = [-1, 1]$.

Q.5 Let $A = \{1, 2\}$, $B = \{a, b, c\}$. A function is defined from A to B. What is the number of possible onto functions?

Ans Since, $n(A) < n(B)$, so there is no onto function possible from A to B.

Q.6 Let $f : R \rightarrow R$ defined by $f(x) = \text{sgn}(x)$. Check whether $f(x)$ is one-one and onto.

Ans We know that,

$$\text{sgn}(x) = \begin{cases} -1, & x < 0 \\ 0, & x = 0 \\ 1, & x > 1 \end{cases}$$

So, $f(x)$ is neither one-one nor onto.

Q.7 Give an example of a bijective function.

Ans $f : R \rightarrow R$ defined by $f(x) = x$.

Activity 5

OBJECTIVE

To draw the graph of $\sin^{-1} x$, using the graph of $\sin x$ and demonstrate the concept of mirror reflection (about the line $y = x$).

Material Required

Cardboard, white chart paper, scale, coloured pens, gum, pencil, eraser, cutter, some nails and some thin wires.

Prerequisite Knowledge

1. Concept of inverse of a function.
2. Concept of mirror reflection.

Method of Construction

1. Take a cardboard of suitable dimensions, say, 40 cm × 40 cm.
2. On the cardboard, fix a white chart paper of size 30 cm × 30 cm (say) using gum.
3. On the paper, draw two lines, perpendicular to each other and name them $X'OX$ and YOY' representing the rectangular axes [see given Figure 5.1].
4. Graduate the axes approximately as shown in figure by taking unit on X-axis = 1.25 times the unit of Y-axis.

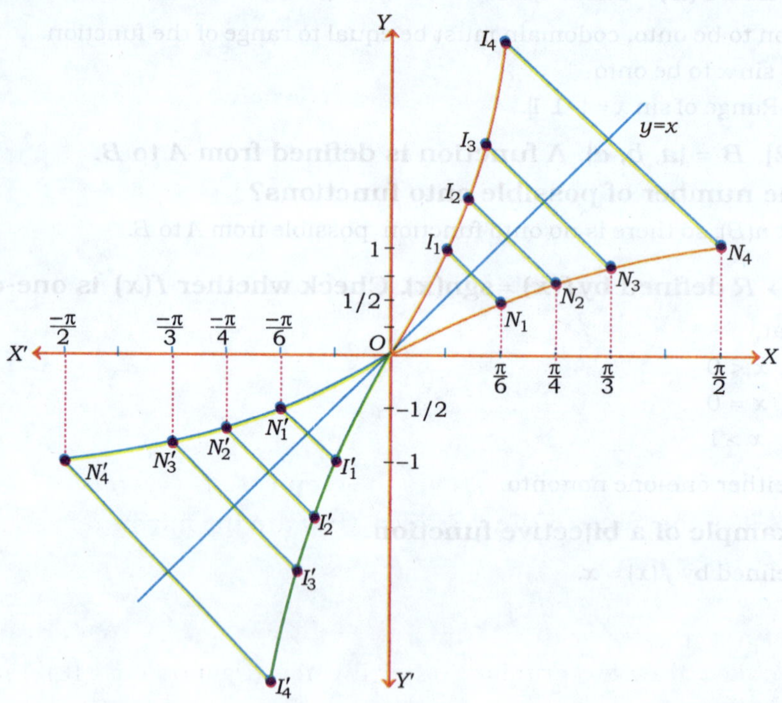

Fig. 5.1

5. Mark the points (approximately) $\left(\frac{\pi}{6}, \sin\frac{\pi}{6}\right), \left(\frac{\pi}{4}, \sin\frac{\pi}{4}\right), ..., \left(\frac{\pi}{2}, \sin\frac{\pi}{2}\right)$ in the coordinate plane.

   Also, fix a nail at each point and name them N_1, N_2, N_3, N_4.

6. Repeat the above process on the other side of the X-axis, marking the points $\left(-\frac{\pi}{6}, \sin\frac{-\pi}{6}\right), \left(\frac{-\pi}{4}, \sin\frac{-\pi}{4}\right), ..., \left(\frac{-\pi}{2}, \sin\frac{-\pi}{2}\right)$ approximately and fix nails on these points as N_1', N_2', N_3', N_4'. At O also, fix a nail.

7. With the help of wire join the nail on both sides of X-axis to get the graph of $\sin x$ from $\frac{-\pi}{2}$ to $\frac{\pi}{2}$.

8. Draw the graph of the line $y = x$ by plotting the points (1, 1), (2, 2), (3, 3), ... etc. At these points fix a wire.

9. From the nails N_1, N_2, N_3, N_4, draw perpendicular on the line $y = x$ and produce these lines such that length of perpendicular on both sides of the line $y = x$ are equal. Name them I_1, I_2, I_3, I_4 and fix nails at these points.

10. Similarly, repeat the above step on the other side of X-axis and fix nails at I_1', I_2', I_3', I_4'.

11. Join the nails on both sides of the line $y = x$ by a tight wire. The curve so obtained shows the graph of $y = \sin^{-1} x$.

Demonstration

Put a mirror on the line $y = x$. The image of the graph of $\sin x$ in the mirror will represent the graph of $\sin^{-1} x$ showing that $\sin^{-1} x$ is mirror reflection of $\sin x$ and *vice-versa*.

Observation

The image of point N_1 in the mirror (the line $y = x$) is ....

The image of point N_2 in the mirror (the line $y = x$) is ....

The image of point N_3 in the mirror (the line $y = x$) is ....

The image of point N_4 in the mirror (the line $y = x$) is ....

The image of point N_1' in the mirror (the line $y = x$) is ....

The image of point N_2' in the mirror (the line $y = x$) is ....

The image of point N_3' in the mirror (the line $y = x$) is ....

The image of point N_4' in the mirror (the line $y = x$) is ....

The image of the graph of $\sin x$ in $y = x$ is the graph of .... and the image of the graph of $\sin^{-1} x$ in $y = x$ is the graph of ....

Result

The image of the graph of $\sin x$ in the line $y = x$ is the graph of $\sin^{-1} x$ and the image of the graph of $\sin^{-1} x$ in the line $y = x$ is the graph of $\sin x$. Hence, they are the mirror reflection of each other in the line $y = x$.

Application

In the same way we can draw the graph of other inverse trigonometric functions i.e. $\cos^{-1} x$, $\tan^{-1} x$ etc.

Necessary Concepts Related to Activity

1. Inverse of a Function

Let $f : A \to B$ be a bijection. Then, a function $g : B \to A$ which associates each element $y \in B$ to a unique element $x \in A$ such that $f(x) = y$ is called the inverse of f. i.e. $f(x) = y \Leftrightarrow g(y) = x$

The inverse of f is generally denoted by f^{-1}.

Thus, if $f : A \to B$ is bijection, then $f^{-1} : B \to A$ is such that $f(x) = y \Leftrightarrow f^{-1}(y) = x$

2. Mirror Reflection

The graph of a bijection f and its inverse f^{-1} are related to each other. If (a, b) is a point on the graph of f, then $b = f(a)$ and $a = f^{-1}(b)$. As, $b \in$ domain of f^{-1}, therefore $(b, f^{-1}(b))$ is a point on the graph of f^{-1}. But, $(b, f^{-1}(b)) = (b, a)$. Therefore, (b, a) also lies on the graph of f^{-1}. Thus, if (a, b) is a point on the graph of f, then (b, a) is a point on the graph of f^{-1}. But, (a, b) and (b, a) are reflections of one another in the line $y = x$. Thus, the graph of f^{-1} may be obtained by reflecting the graph of f in the line mirror $y = x$. So, the graphs of f and f^{-1} are mirror images of each other in the line mirror $y = x$.

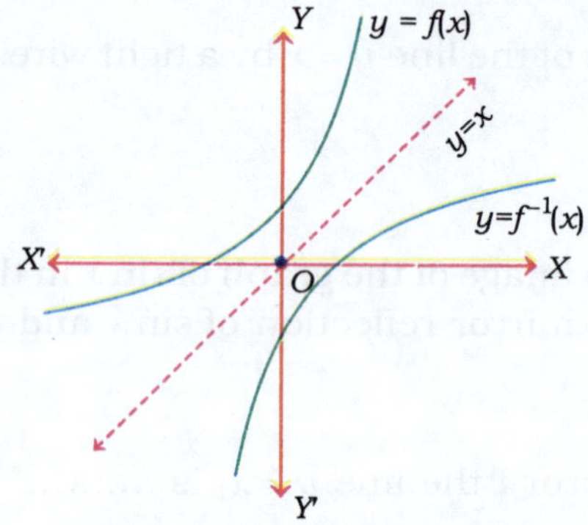

Fig. 5.2

Viva-Voce

Q.1 Define inverse of a function.

Ans Let $f : A \to B$ be a bijection. Then, a function $g : B \to A$, which associates each element $y \in B$ to a unique element $x \in A$ such that $f(x) = y$ is called the inverse of f.

Q.2 What is the domain of $\sin^{-1} x$?

Ans Domain of $\sin^{-1} x$ is $[-1, 1]$.

Q.3 What is the range of $\sin^{-1} x$?

Ans Range of $\sin^{-1} x$ is $\left[\frac{-\pi}{2}, \frac{\pi}{2}\right]$.

Q.4 What is the relation between the graphs of a function and its inverse.

Ans The graphs of a function and its inverse are mirror images of each other in the line $y = x$.

Q.5 The period of sin x is ....

Ans sin x has a period of 2π.

Q.6 If $\sin^{-1}(\sin x) = x$, then x belongs to ....

Ans $x \in \left[-\frac{\pi}{2}, \frac{\pi}{2}\right]$

Q.7 What is the basic condition of inverse mapping?

Ans One-one onto mappings possess inverse mapping.

Q.8 Write the difference between maximum and minimum values of $\sin^{-1} x$ for $x \in [-1, 1]$.

Ans π

Activity 6

OBJECTIVE

To explore the principal value of the function $\sin^{-1} x$ using a unit circle.

Material Required

Cardboard, white chart sheet, string, ruler, glue, steel wires and needle.

Prerequisite knowledge

1. Concept of inverse of a function
2. Concept of inverse of sine functions
3. Concept of principal value

Method of Construction

1. Take a cardboard of a suitable size and paste a white chart sheet on it.
2. Draw a unit circle with centre O on it.
3. From the centre of the circle, draw two perpendicular lines $X'OX$ and YOY' representing X-axis and Y-axis respectively as shown in Figure 6.1.

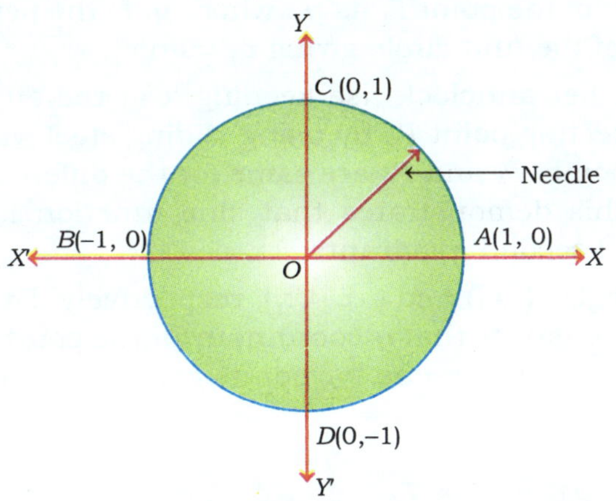

Fig. 6.1

4. Denote the points $A(1, 0)$, $B(-1, 0)$, $C(0, 1)$ and $D(0, -1)$, where the circle cuts the X-axis and Y-axis respectively as shown in Figure 6.1.
5. Fix two strings on opposite sides of the cardboard which are parallel to the Y-axis. Fix one steel wire between the strings such that the wire can be moved parallel to X-axis as shown in Figure 6.2.

6. Take a needle of unit length. Fix one end of it at the centre of the circle and allow the other end to move freely along the circle.

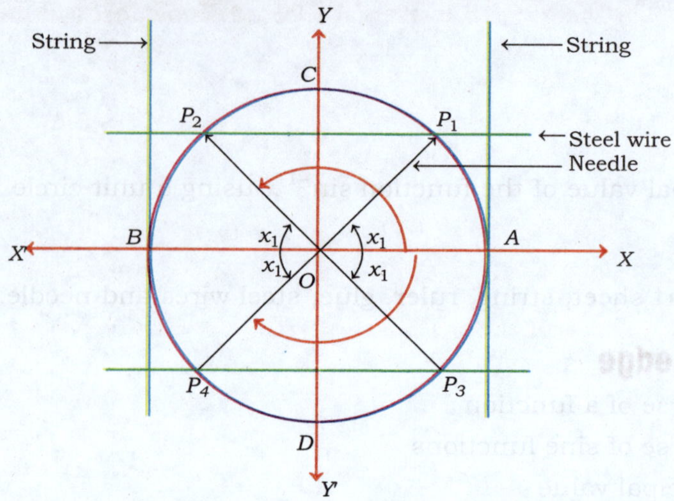

Fig. 6.2

Demonstration

1. Keep the needle at an arbitrary angle say x_1 with the positive direction of X-axis. Measure of angle in radian is equal to the length of intercepted arc of the unit circle.
2. Slide the steel wire between the string, parallel to X-axis such that the wire meets with the free end of the needle (say P_1) Figure 6.2.
3. Mark the y-coordinate of the point P_1 as y_1, where y_1 is the perpendicular distance of steel wire from the X-axis of the unit circle giving $y_1 = \sin x_1$.
4. Rotate the needle further anticlockwise keeping it at the angle $(\pi - x)$. Find the value of y-coordinate of intersecting point P_2 by using sliding steel wire. We find that the value of y-coordinate for the points P_1 and P_2 are same for the different value of angles, $y_1 = \sin x_1$ and $y_1 = \sin(\pi - x_1)$. This demonstrates that sine function is not one-to-one for angles considered in first and second quadrants.
5. Keep the needle at angles $(-x_1)$ and $(-\pi + x_1)$, respectively. By sliding down the steel wire parallel to X-axis, demonstrate that y-coordinate for the points P_3 and P_4 are the same and thus sine function is not one-to-one for points considered in 3rd and 4th quadrants as shown in Figure 6.2.

6. The y-coordinate of the points P_3 and P_1 are different. Move the needle in anti-clockwise direction starting from $-\frac{\pi}{2}$ to $\frac{\pi}{2}$ and observe the behaviour of y-coordinates of points P_5, P_6, P_7 and P_8 by sliding the steel wire parallel to X-axis accordingly. y-coordinate of points P_5, P_6, P_7 and P_8 are different (see Figure 6.3).

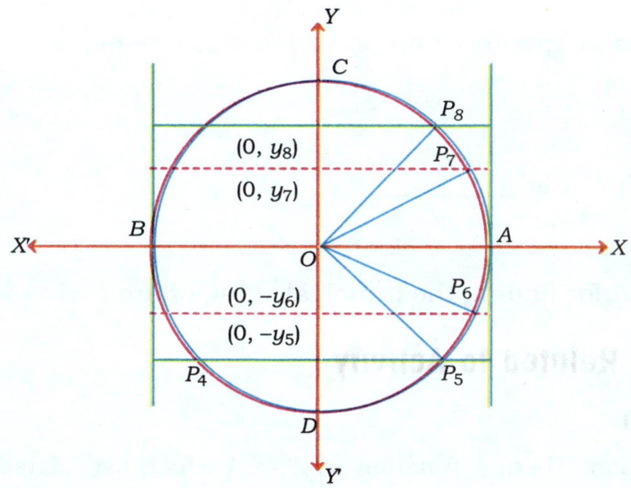

Fig. 6.3

Hence, sine function is one-one in the domain $\left[-\frac{\pi}{2}, \frac{\pi}{2}\right]$ and its range lies between -1 and 1.

7. Keep the needle at any arbitrary angle (say θ) lying in the interval $\left[-\frac{\pi}{2}, \frac{\pi}{2}\right]$ and denote the y-coordinate of the intersecting point P_9 as y. (see Figure 6.4). Then, $y = \sin\theta$ or $\theta = \sin^{-1} y$ as sine function is one-one and onto in the domain $\left[-\frac{\pi}{2}, \frac{\pi}{2}\right]$ and range $[-1, 1]$. So, its inverse exist. The domain of $\sin^{-1} x$ function is $[-1, 1]$ and range is $\left[-\frac{\pi}{2}, \frac{\pi}{2}\right]$. This range is called the principal value of $\sin^{-1} x$ function.

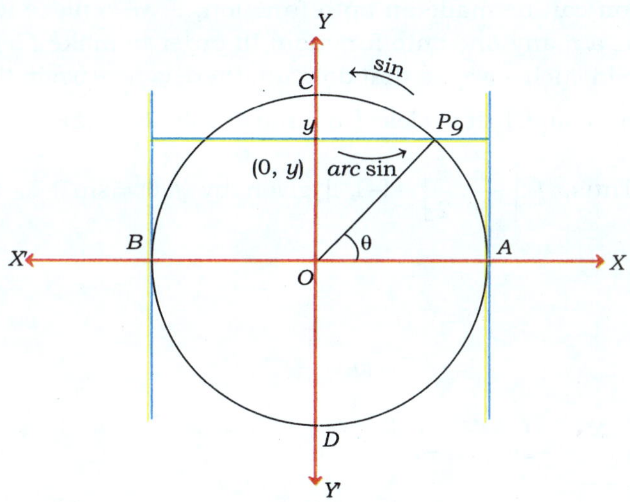

Fig. 6.4

Observations

1. Sine function is non-negative in .... and .... quadrants.
2. For the quadrants 3rd and 4th, sine function is ....
3. $\theta = \sin^{-1} y \Rightarrow y =$ .... θ, where $-\frac{\pi}{2} \le \theta \le$ ....
4. The other domains of sine function on which it is one-one and onto provides .... for $\sin^{-1} x$ function.

Result

The principle value of $\sin^{-1} x$ is __________

Application

This activity can be used for finding the principal value of arc cosine function ($\cos^{-1} x$).

Necessary Concepts Related to Activity

1. Inverse of a Function

Let $f : A \to B$ be a bijection. Then, a function $g : B \to A$ which associates each element $y \in B$ to a unique element $x \in A$ such that $f(x) = y$ is called the inverse of f. i.e. $f(x) = y \Leftrightarrow g(y) = x$.

The inverse of f is generally denoted by f^{-1}.

Thus, if $f : A \to B$ is bijection, then $f^{-1} : B \to A$ is such that $f(x) = y \Leftrightarrow f^{-1}(y) = x$.

We know that trigonometric functions are periodic functions, and hence, in general, all trigonometric functions are not bijective, consequently their inverse do not exist. However, if we restrict their domains and codomains, they can be made bijective and we can obtain their inverses.

2. Inverse of Sine Functions

Consider the function $f : R \to R$ given by $f(x) = \sin x$. The graph of this function is shown in Figure 6.5. Clearly, it is a many-one function and not an onto function as its range $[-1, 1]$ is not the same as its codomain.

We know that any function can be made an onto function, if we replace its codomain by its range. Therefore, $f : R \to [-1, 1]$ is a many-one onto function. In order to make f a one-one function, we will have to restrict its domain in such a way in that domain, there is no turn in the graph and the function takes every value between -1 and 1. It is clear from the graph, if we take the domain as $\left[-\frac{\pi}{2}, \frac{\pi}{2}\right]$, then $f(x)$ becomes one-one. Thus, $f : \left[-\frac{\pi}{2}, \frac{\pi}{2}\right] \to [-1, 1]$ given by $f(\theta) = \sin\theta$ is a bijective and hence is invertible.

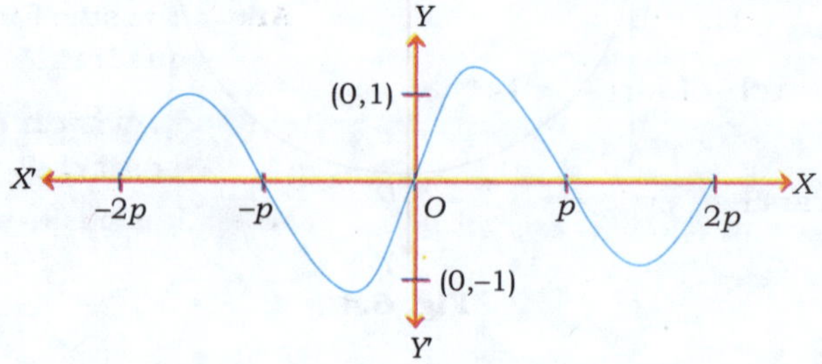

Fig. 6.5

Graph of $\sin^{-1} x : [-1, 1] \rightarrow \left(-\frac{\pi}{2}, \frac{\pi}{2}\right)$ is given as

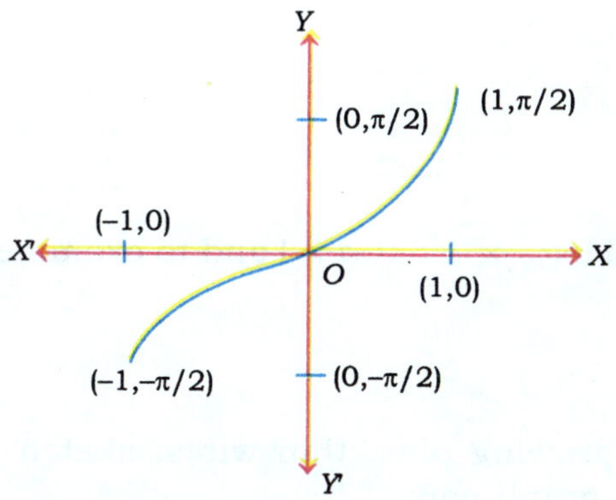

Fig. 6.6

Principle Value

In the above discussion, we have restricted the domain of sine function to the interval $\left[-\frac{\pi}{2}, \frac{\pi}{2}\right]$ to make it a bijection. Infact, if we restrict its domain to any one of the intervals $\left[-\frac{\pi}{2}, \frac{\pi}{2}\right], \left[\frac{\pi}{2}, \frac{3\pi}{2}\right], \left[\frac{3\pi}{2}, \frac{5\pi}{2}\right]$, $\left[-\frac{3\pi}{2}, -\frac{\pi}{2}\right]$ or in general $\left[n\pi - \frac{\pi}{2}, n\pi + \frac{\pi}{2}\right]$, $n \in z$, then also it becomes a bijection. We can, therefore, define the inverse of the sine function in each of these intervals. Thus, $\sin^{-1} x$ is a function with domain [–1, 1] and range $\left[-\frac{\pi}{2}, \frac{\pi}{2}\right]$ or $\left[-\frac{3\pi}{2}, -\frac{\pi}{2}\right]$ or $\left[\frac{\pi}{2}, \frac{3\pi}{2}\right]$ and so on and corresponding to each such interval, we get a branch of the function $\sin^{-1} x$. The branch of the function $\sin^{-1} x : [-1, 1] \rightarrow \left[-\frac{\pi}{2}, \frac{\pi}{2}\right]$, is called the principal value branch and the value corresponding to it is called the principal value.

Viva-Voce

Q.1 The principal value of $\sin^{-1}\left(\frac{-\sqrt{3}}{2}\right)$ is ....

Ans $\sin^{-1}\left(\frac{-\sqrt{3}}{2}\right) = \theta \Rightarrow \sin\theta = \frac{-\sqrt{3}}{2}$

$\Rightarrow \sin\theta = \sin\left(\frac{-\pi}{3}\right) \Rightarrow \theta = \frac{-\pi}{3}$.

Q.2 Principal value branch of $\sin^{-1} x$ is ....

Ans The principal value branch of $\sin^{-1} x$ is $\left[\frac{-\pi}{2}, \frac{\pi}{2}\right]$.

Q.3 The value of $\sin^{-1} x \rightarrow \left[\frac{-\pi}{2}, \frac{\pi}{2}\right]$ is ....

Ans The value of $\sin^{-1} x \rightarrow \left[\frac{-\pi}{2}, \frac{\pi}{2}\right]$ is [–1, 1], which is called the principal value.

Q.4 Sine function is negative in ....

Ans The sine function is negative in IIIrd and IVth quadrant.

Q.5 In which quadrant, sine function positive?

Ans It is positive in the Ist and IInd quadrants.

Activity 7

OBJECTIVE

To sketch the graphs of a^x and $\log_a x$, $a > 0$, $a \neq 1$ and to examine that they are mirror images of each other.

Material Required

Cardboard, geometrical box, drawing pins, thin wires, sketch pens, thick white sheet, glue, pencil, eraser, a plane mirror, graph paper.

Prerequisite Knowledge

1. Concept of logarithm.
2. Concept of graph of $\log x$ and a^x.

Method of Construction

1. On the cardboard, fix a thick paper sheet of size 20 cm × 20 cm (say) and paste a graph sheet on it.

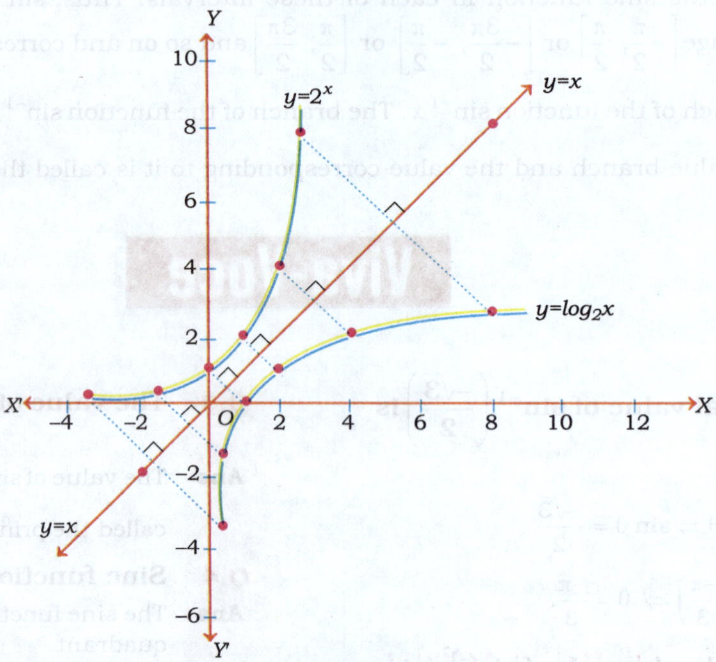

Fig. 7.1

2. On the sheet, draw two perpendicular lines *XOX'* and *YOY'*, representing coordinate axes.
3. Denote graduations on the two axes as shown in the above Figure 7.1.
4. Plot some ordered pairs satisfying $y = a^x$ and $y = \log_a x$. Mark these ordered pairs and join them by free hand curves in both the cases and fix thin pieces of wires along these curves with the help of drawing pins.
5. Draw the graph of $y = x$, and fix a wire along this graph, using drawing pins.

Demonstration

1. For a^x, take $a = 2$ (say), and find ordered pairs satisfying it as

x	0	1	-1	2	-2	3	-3	$\frac{1}{2}$	$-\frac{1}{2}$	4
2^x	1	2	0.5	4	$\frac{1}{4}$	8	$\frac{1}{8}$	1.4	0.7	16

and plot these ordered pairs on the graph paper and fix a drawing pin at each point.

2. Join the bases of drawing pins with a thin wire. This will represent the graph of 2^x.
3. Now, let $y = \log_2 x$ or $x = 2^y$. Some ordered pair satisfying it are

x	1	2	$\frac{1}{2}$	4	$\frac{1}{4}$	8	$\frac{1}{8}$
y	0	1	-1	2	-2	3	-3

Plot these ordered pairs on the graph paper and fix a drawing pin at each plotted point. Join the bases of the drawing pins with a thin wire. This will represent the graph of $\log_2 x$.

4. Draw the graph of line $y = x$ on the graph paper and fix a wire along it.
5. Place a mirror along the wire representing $y = x$. It can be observed that the two graphs of the given functions are mirror images of each other in the line $y = x$.

Observations

1. Image of ordered pair (1, 2) on the graph of $y = 2^x$ in $y = x$ is ______. It lies on the graph of $y =$ _______.
2. Image of the point (4, 2) on the graph $y = \log_2 x$ in $y = x$ is _________ which lies on the graph of $y =$_______.

Repeat this process for some more points lying on the two graphs.

Result

The graph of $y = 2^x$ and $y = \log_2 x$ are mirror images of each other.

Application

This activity is useful to understand the concept of exponential and logarithmic function which are mirror images of each other in $y = x$.

Suggested Activity

Do same activity for $y = 5^x$ and $\log_5 x$.

Necessary Concepts Related to Activity

1. Logarithmic Function

If a is a positive real number, other than 1 and x is a rational number such that $a^x = N$, then we can say that logarithm of N to base a is x or x is the logarithm of N to the base a, written as $\log_a N = x$.

Thus, $$a^x = N \Leftrightarrow \log_a N = x$$

In other words, the function from positive real numbers to real numbers is defined as $\log_a : R^+ \to R \Rightarrow \log_a(x) = y$, if $a^y = x$, is called logarithmic function.

2. Graph of Logarithm

(i) The graph of $y = \log_a x$, $a > 1$ is

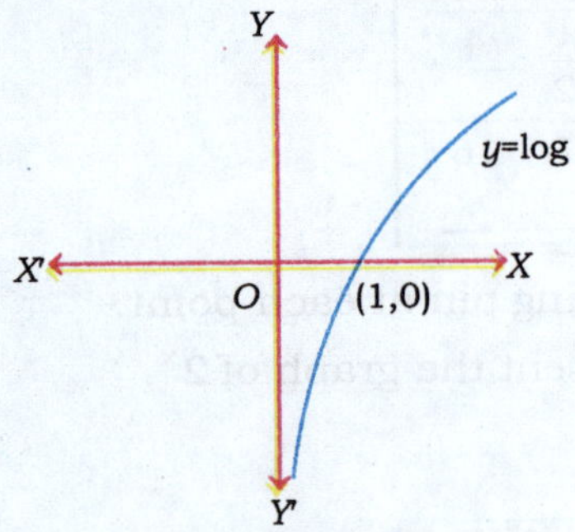

Fig. 7.2

(ii) The graph of $y = \log_a x$, $0 < a < 1$ is

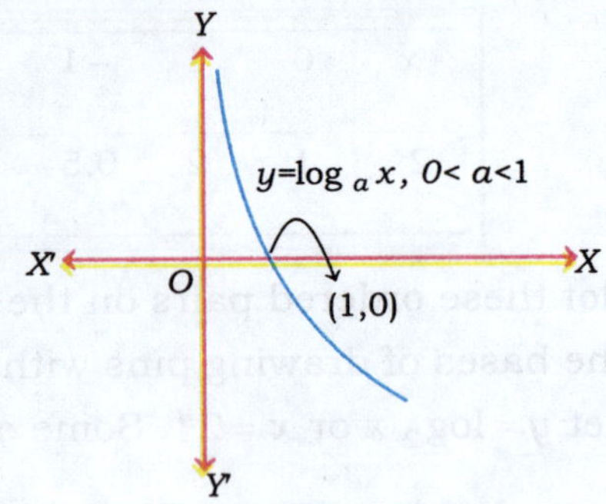

Fig. 7.3

3. Graph of a^x

(i) The graph of $y = a^x$, $a > 1$

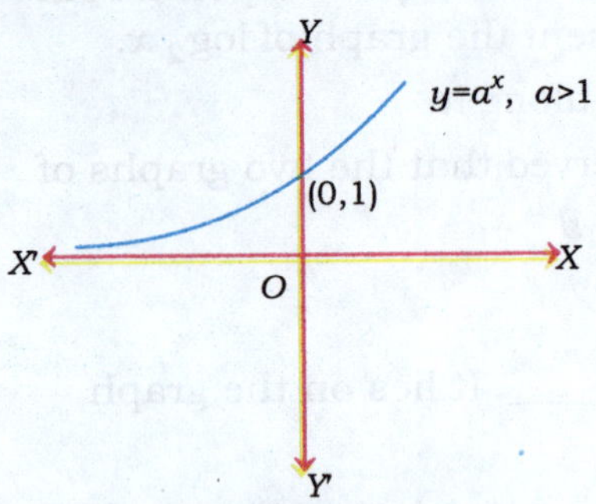

Fig. 7.4

(ii) The graph of $y = a^x$, $0 < a < 1$

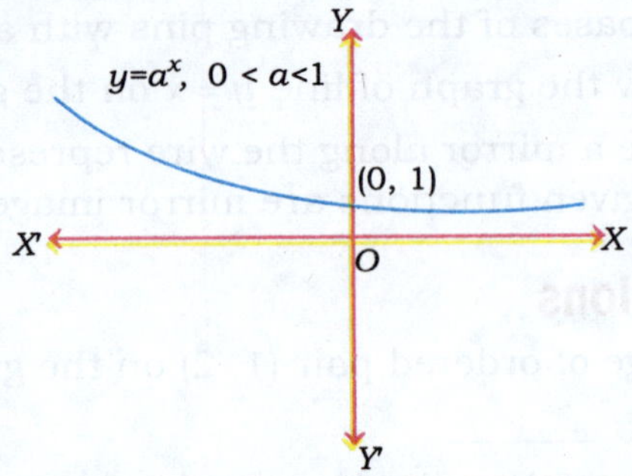

Fig. 7.5

Viva-Voce

Q.1 If the graphs of two functions are mirror image of each other under the line $y = x$, then what is relation between them?

Ans They are inverse of each other.

Q.2 If f is an invertible function, then what is the value of $(f^{-1})^{-1}$?

Ans $(f^{-1})^{-1} = f$

Q.3 Write the relation between a^x and $\log_a x$.

Ans Both are inverse to each other.

Q.4 The domain of $\log_a x$ is ....

Ans Its domain consists of positive real numbers.

Q.5 What are the necessary condition for a function to be invertible?

Ans For a function to be invertible, it must be injective and surjective, i.e. bijective.

Q.6 Range of $\log_a x$ is ....

Ans Its range is set of all real numbers.

Q.7 When the logarithmic function is defined.

Ans The logarithmic function $\log_a x$ is defined when $x > 0$, $a > 0$ and $a \neq 1$.

Activity 8

OBJECTIVE

To establish a relationship between common logarithm (to the base 10) and natural logarithm (to the base *e*) of the number *x*.

Material Required

Cardboard, white sheet, graph paper, pencil, scale, log tables or calculator (graphic/scientific).

Prerequisite Knowledge

1. Concept of common logarithm.
2. Concept of natural logarithm.

Method of Construction

1. Fix a graph paper on a white sheet and paste it on the cardboard.
2. Draw two perpendicular lines XOX', $Y'OY$ with O as origin representing coordinate axes.
3. Find some ordered pairs satisfying the function $y = \log_{10} x$, using log tables or calculator and draw the graph of the function on the graph paper (see Figure 8.1).

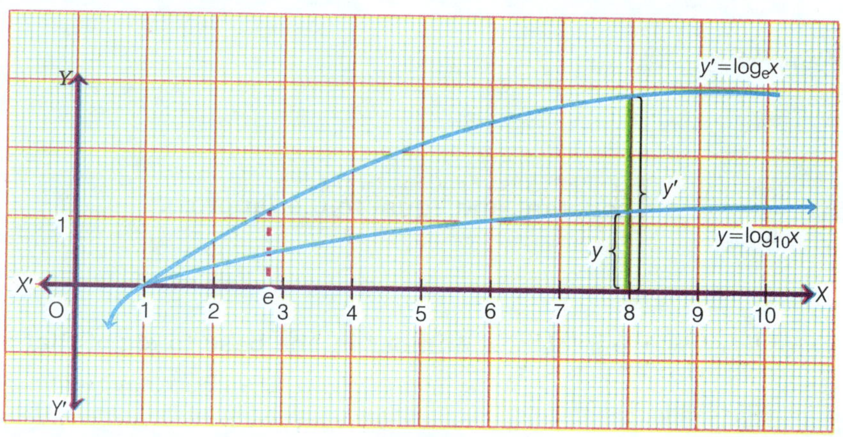

Fig. 8.1

4. Similarly, using log table or calculator, draw the graph of $y' = \log_e x$ on the same graph paper as shown in the Figure 8.1.

Demonstration

1. Take any point on the positive direction of *X*-axis and write its *x*-coordinate.
2. For this value of *x*, using a scale find the value of *y*-coordinates for both the graphs of $y = \log_{10} x$ and $y' = \log_e x$ by actual measurement and record them as *y* and *y'*, respectively.
3. Find the ratio $\frac{y}{y'}$.

4. Repeat the above steps for some more points on the X-axis and find the corresponding ratios of the ordinates as in Step 3.
5. Each of these ratios will nearly be the same and equal to 0.4, which is approximately equal to $\frac{1}{\log_e 10}$.

Observations

1.

S.No.	Points on the X-axis	$y = \log_{10} x$	$y' = \log_e x$	Ratio $\frac{y}{y'}$ (approximate)
1.	$x_1 =$	$y_1 =$	$y_1' =$	....
2.	$x_2 =$	$y_2 =$	$y_2' =$	....
3.	$x_3 =$	$y_3 =$	$y_3' =$	....
4.	$x_4 =$	$y_4 =$	$y_4' =$	....
5.	$x_5 =$	$y_5 =$	$y_5' =$	....
6.	$x_6 =$	$y_6 =$	$y_6' =$	....

2. The value of $\frac{y}{y'}$ for each point x is equal to ________ (approximately)
3. The observed value of $\frac{y}{y'}$ in each case is approximately equal to the value of $\frac{1}{\log_e 10}$. (Yes/No)
4. Therefore, $\log_{10} e = \frac{1}{\log_e 10}$

Result

We have found that $\frac{\log_{10} x}{\log_e x}$ is a constant and equal to 0.4 (approx).

Application

This activity is useful in converting log of a number in one base to log of that same number in another base.

Note Let $y = \log_{10} x$ or $x = 10^y$

Taking logarithm to base e on both the sides, we get

$$\log_e x = y \log_e 10 \text{ or } y = \frac{1}{\log_e 10}(\log_e x)$$

$$\Rightarrow \frac{\log_{10} x}{\log_e x} = \frac{1}{\log_e 10} = 0.434294 \text{ (using log tables/calculator).}$$

Necessary Concepts Related to Activity

Generally two systems of logarithms are used

1. Common Logarithms

In this system, the base is always taken to be 10. It is very useful in all practical calculations. If no base is mentioned, the base is always taken as 10.

e.g. log 2 means $\log_{10} 2$.

We have, $\log 10 = \log_{10} 10 = 1$, $\log 10000 = \log_{10} 10000 = 4$ etc.

2. Natural Logarithms

In this system, the base of the logarithm is taken as e, where e is an irrational number lying between 2 and 3. The approximate value of e is 2.72. The value of e is given by

$$e = 1 + \frac{1}{1!} + \frac{1}{2!} + \frac{1}{3!} + \frac{1}{4!} + \dots$$

It is also denoted as $\ln x$ or $\log_e x$.

Viva-Voce

Q.1 Define common logarithm.

Ans All logarithm to the base 10 are known as common logarithm. It is also known as decimal log.

Q.2 Define natural logarithm.

Ans All logarithm to the base e are known as natural logarithm. It is denoted as $\log_e$ or ln.

Q.3 What is the value of e?

Ans $e \cong 2.718281828 4590459$ or $e \cong 2.72$.

Q.4 Which is greater $\log_{10} 2$ or $\log_e 2$?

Ans We know that, $\dfrac{\log_{10} x}{\log_e x} = 0.4$

Put $x = 2$, $\dfrac{\log_{10} 2}{\log_e 2} = 0.4$

$\therefore \log_{10} 2 = 0.4 \times \log_e 2$

Hence, $\log_e 2 > \log_{10} 2$

Q.5 What is the value of $\log_e e$?

Ans $\log_e e = 1$ $\quad [\because \log_a a = 1]$

Q.6 What is the value of $\log_{10} e$?

Ans $\log_{10} e = \dfrac{1}{\log_e 10} = 0.4$

Activity 9

OBJECTIVE

To find analytically the limit of a function $f(x)$ at $x = c$ and also to check the continuity of the function at that point.

Material Required

Paper, pencil, calculator.

Prerequisite Knowledge

1. Concept of left hand and right hand limit of a function.
2. Concept of continuity of a function at a point.

Method of Construction

1. Consider the function given by $f(x) = \begin{cases} \dfrac{x^2 - 9}{x - 3}, & x \neq 3 \\ 7, & x = 3 \end{cases}$
2. Take some points on the left side and some points on the right side of $c (= 3)$, which are very near to c.
3. Calculate the corresponding values of $f(x)$ for each of the points considered in above step.
4. Record the values of points on the left side and right side of c as x and the corresponding values of $f(x)$ in a form of a table.

Demonstration

The values of x and $f(x)$ are recorded as follows

1. **Table 1** For points on the left of $c (= 3)$

x	2.9	2.99	2.999	2.9999	2.99999	2.999999	2.9999999
$f(x)$	5.9	5.99	5.999	5.9999	5.99999	5.99999	5.9999999

2. **Table 2** For points on the right of $c (= 3)$

x	3.1	3.01	3.001	3.0001	3.00001	3.000001	3.0000001
$f(x)$	6.1	6.01	6.001	6.0001	6.00001	6.000001	6.0000001

Observations

1. The value of $f(x)$ is approaching to ...., as $x \to 3$ from the left.
2. The value of $f(x)$ is approaching to ...., as $x \to 3$ from the right.
3. So, $\lim_{x \to 3^-} f(x) =$ .... and $\lim_{x \to 3^+} f(x) =$ ....
4. Therefore, $\lim_{x \to 3} f(x) =$ ...., $f(3) =$......
5. Is $\lim_{x \to 3} f(x) = f(3)$ ...... ? (Yes/No)
6. Since, $f(c) \neq \lim_{x \to 3} f(x)$, so the function is .... at $x = 3$ (continuous/not continuous).

Result

This activity is very helpful in understanding the existence of limit of a function at a point and check its continuity.

Application

From the above activity we can easily understand the basic concept of limit and continuity of a function at a given point.

Necessary Concepts Related to Activity

1. Definition of Limit

If x approaches a, $(x \to a)$, $f(x)$ approaches l, $(f(x) \to l)$, where l is a real number, then l is called limit of the function $f(x)$. In symbolic form, it can be written as $\lim_{x \to a} f(x) = l$.

2. Left Hand Limit (LHL)

$\lim_{x \to a^-} f(x)$ is the expected value of f at $x = a$ given the value of f near x to the left of a.
This value is called the left hand limit of $f(x)$ at $x = a$,

i.e. LHL $= \lim_{x \to a^-} f(x) = \lim_{h \to 0} f(a - h)$, where h is very small and $h > 0$.

3. Right Hand Limit (RHL)

$\lim_{x \to a^+} f(x)$ is the expected value of f at $x = a$ given the value of f near x to the right of a. This value is called the right hand limit of $f(x)$ at $x = a$,
i.e. RHL $= \lim_{x \to a^+} f(x) = \lim_{h \to 0} f(a + h)$, where h is very small and $h > 0$.

4. Existence of Limit

If both the left hand limit and the right hand limit exist (i.e. finite and unique) and coincide (i.e. same), then we can say that limit exists and the common value l (say) is called the limit of $f(x)$ at $x = a$, i.e. if $\lim_{x \to a^-} f(x) = \lim_{x \to a^+} f(x) = l$, then we say that $\lim_{x \to a} f(x)$ exists and we write $\lim_{x \to a} f(x) = l$.

5. Continuity of a Function at a Point

A function $f(x)$ is said to be continuous at a point $x = a$ of its domain, iff $\lim_{x \to a} f(x) = f(a)$.

Thus, $f(x)$ is continuous at $x = a \Leftrightarrow \lim_{x \to a} f(x) = f(a) \Leftrightarrow \lim_{x \to a^-} f(x) = \lim_{x \to a^+} f(x) = f(a)$.

Viva-Voce

Q.1 What is the necessary condition for limit to exist?

Ans For a function at $x = a$, limit will exist, if left hand limit is equal to right hand limit. i.e. LHL = RHL

Q.2 What is the value of $\lim_{x \to 4^-} [x]$?

Ans $\lim_{x \to 4^-} [x] = \lim_{h \to 0} [4 - h] = [4 - 0] = 4$

Q.3 What is the value $\lim_{x \to 4^+} [x]$?

Ans $\lim_{x \to 4^+} [x] = \lim_{h \to 0} [4 + h] = 4$

Q.4 Check whether $\lim_{x \to 0} \frac{|x|}{x}$ exists or not.

Ans $\text{LHL} = \lim_{x \to 0^-} \frac{|x|}{x} = \lim_{h \to 0} \frac{|0 - h|}{0 - h} = \lim_{h \to 0} \frac{h}{-h} = -1$

and $\text{RHL} = \lim_{x \to 0^+} \frac{|x|}{x} = \lim_{h \to 0} \frac{|0 + h|}{0 + h} = \lim_{h \to 0} \frac{h}{h} = 1$

Since, LHL $\neq$ RHL, so limit does not exist.

Q.5 What is $x \to a^-$ equivalent to?

Ans $x \to a^-$ is equivalent to $x = a - h$, where $h \to 0$

Q.6 What is $x \to a^+$ equivalent to?

Ans $x \to a^+$ is equivalent to $x = a + h$, where $h \to 0$

Q.7 What is the necessary condition for a function to be continuous at a given point?

Ans A function $f(x)$ is said to be continuous at a point $x = a$ of its domain, iff $\lim_{x \to a} f(x) = f(a)$.

Q.8 State whether, if $f(x)$ and $g(x)$ are continuous at $x = a$, then $(f + g)(x)$ is also continuous at $x = a$ or not.

Ans Yes. Since, f and g are continuous at $x = a$.

Then $\lim_{x \to a} f(x) = f(a)$ and $\lim_{x \to a} g(x) = g(a)$.

$$\therefore \lim_{x \to a} (f + g)(x) = \lim_{x \to a} [f(x) + g(x)]$$

$$= \lim_{x \to a} f(x) + \lim_{x \to a} g(x)$$

$$= f(a) + g(a)$$

$$= (f + g)(a)$$

Activity 10

OBJECTIVE

To verify that for a function f to be continuous at given point x_0, $\Delta y = |f(x_0 + \Delta x) - f(x_0)|$ is arbitrarily small, provided Δx is sufficiently small.

Material Required

Cardboard, some white sheets, pencil, scale, calculator, gum.

Prerequisite Knowledge

Concept of continuity of a function at a point.

Method of Construction

1. Paste a white sheet on the cardboard.
2. Consider a function $y^2 = 4ax$ and draw the curve of this function on the white sheet as shown in Figure 10.1.

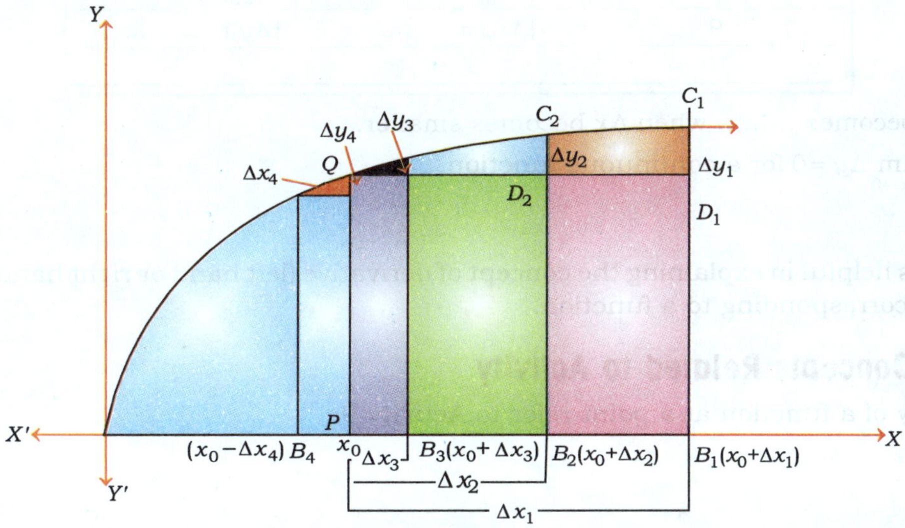

Fig. 10.1

Demonstration

1. Take any point $P(x_0, 0)$ on the positive side of X-axis and corresponding to this point, mark the point $Q(x_0, y_0)$ on the curve.
2. Take one more point $B_1(x_0 + \Delta x_1, 0)$ to the right of P, where Δx_1 is an increment in x.
3. Draw the perpendicular from B_1 and let it cut the curve at C_1. Let the coordinates of C_1 be $(x_0 + \Delta x_1, y_0 + \Delta y_1)$.
4. Draw a perpendicular from the point $Q(x_0, y_0)$ to meet C_1B_1 at D_1.

5. Now, measure $PB_1 = \Delta x_1$ (say) and record it and also measure $C_1D_1 = \Delta y_1$ and record it.
6. Reduce the increment in x to Δx_2 (i.e. $\Delta x_2 < \Delta x_1$) to get another point B_2 $(x_0 + \Delta x_2, 0)$. Get the corresponding point C_2 on the curve.
7. Let the perpendicular QD_1 intersects C_2B_2 at D_2.
8. Again, measure $PB_2 = \Delta x_2$ and record it.
   Measure $C_2D_2 = \Delta y_2$ and record it.
9. Repeat the above steps for some more points so that Δx becomes smaller and smaller.

Observations

1.

S. No.	Value of increment in x_0	Corresponding increment in y
1.	$\lvert\Delta x_1\rvert$ = ...	$\lvert\Delta y_1\rvert$ = ...
2.	$\lvert\Delta x_2\rvert$ = ...	$\lvert\Delta y_2\rvert$ = ...
3.	$\lvert\Delta x_3\rvert$ = ...	$\lvert\Delta y_3\rvert$ = ...
4.	$\lvert\Delta x_4\rvert$ = ...	$\lvert\Delta y_4\rvert$ = ...
5.	$\lvert\Delta x_5\rvert$ = ...	$\lvert\Delta y_5\rvert$ = ...
6.	$\lvert\Delta x_6\rvert$ = ...	$\lvert\Delta y_6\rvert$ = ...
7.	$\lvert\Delta x_7\rvert$ = ...	$\lvert\Delta y_7\rvert$ = ...
8.	$\lvert\Delta x_8\rvert$ = ...	$\lvert\Delta y_8\rvert$ = ...
9.	$\lvert\Delta x_9\rvert$ = ...	$\lvert\Delta y_9\rvert$ = ...
10.		

2. So, Δy becomes .... when Δx becomes smaller.
3. Thus, $\lim_{\Delta x \to 0} \Delta y = 0$ for a continuous function.

Application

This activity is helpful in explaining the concept of derivative (left hand or right hand) at any point on the curve corresponding to a function.

Necessary Concepts Related to Activity

For continuity of a function at a point refer to Activity 9.

Viva-Voce

Q.1 Define diferentiability of a function at a point.

Ans A function is differentiable at a given point if it has a unique tangent at the given point.

Q.2 If Δx is a small change in x and Δy is corresponding change in y, then $\Delta y = f(x + \Delta x) - f(x)$. Is it true or false?

Ans True

Q.3 The differential of y, denoted by dy is defined by dy = ...

Ans $\left(\frac{dy}{dx}\right)\Delta x.$

Q.4 Is every differentiable function continuous?

Ans Yes.

Q.5 Is every continuous function differentiable?

Ans It is not necessary that every continuous function is differentiable.

Q.6 Give an example of a function which is continuous but not differentiable at a point.

Ans $f(x) = |x|$ at $x = 0$ is continuous but not differentiable.

Q.7 If $f(x)$ is differentiable at $x = c$, then write the value of $\lim_{x \to c} f(x)$.

Ans Since, $f(x)$ is differentiable at $x = c$, then it must be continuous at $x = c$.

$\therefore \quad \lim_{x \to c} f(x) = f(c)$

Q.8 $f(x) = x^2$ is discontinuous. Is it true or false?

Ans False

Activity 11

OBJECTIVE

To understand the concepts of decreasing and increasing functions.

Material Required

Some pieces of wire of different lengths, piece of cardboard, white paper, gum, geometry box, trigonometric tables.

Prerequisite Knowledge

1. Concept of increasing function.
2. Concept of decreasing function.

Method of Construction

1. Take a piece of cardboard of a convenient size and using gum paste a white paper on it.
2. Take two pieces of wires of length say 25 cm each and fix them on the white paper to represent the X-axis and Y-axis.
3. Take two more pieces of wire each of suitable length and bend them in the shape of curves representing two functions, fix them on the paper as shown in the given Figure 11.1.

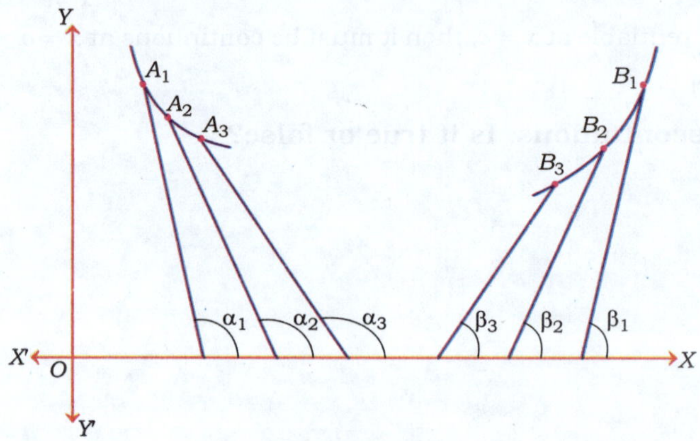

Fig. 11.1

4. Take two straight wires each of suitable length for the purpose of showing tangents to the curves at different points on them.

Demonstration

1. Take one straight wire and place it on the left curve such that it is tangent to the curve at the point say A_1 and making an angle α_1 with the positive direction of X-axis.
2. α_1 is an obtuse angle, so $\tan \alpha_1$ is negative, i.e. the slope of the tangent at A_1 (derivative of the function at A_1) is negative.
3. Take another two points say A_2 and A_3 on the same curve, and make tangents using the same wire, at A_2 and A_3 making angles α_2 and α_3 respectively with the positive direction of X-axis.

4. Here, again α_2 and α_3 are obtuse angles and therefore slopes of the tangents $\tan\alpha_2$ and $\tan\alpha_3$ are both negative i.e. derivatives of the function at A_2 and A_3 are negative.
5. The function given by the left curve is a decreasing function.
6. On the right curve, take three points B_1, B_2, B_3 and using the other straight wire, form tangents at each of these points making angles $\beta_1, \beta_2, \beta_3$ respectively with the positive direction of X-axis, as shown in the Figure 11.1. $\beta_1, \beta_2, \beta_3$ are all acute angles. So, the derivatives of the function at these points are positive. Thus, the function given by the right curve is an increasing function.

Observations

1. α_1 = ________, >90°

   α_2 = ________ > ________,

   α_3 = ________ > ________ ,

   $\tan\alpha_1$ = ________ , (negative)

   $\tan\alpha_2$ = ________ ,(________),

   $\tan\alpha_3$ = ________ ,(________).

   Thus, the function is ________ .

2. β_1 = ________, < 90°,

   β_2 = ________ , <________,

   β_3 = ________ , <________ ,

   $\tan\beta_1$ = ________ ,(positive),

   $\tan\beta_2$ = ________ , (________),

   $\tan\beta_3$ = ________ ,(________).

   Thus, the function is ________ .

Result

We have found points on the curve where the function is decreasing and increasing.

Application

This activity may be useful in explaining the concepts of decreasing and increasing functions.

Necessary Concepts Related to Activity

1. Increasing Function

A function $f(x)$ is said to be a strictly increasing function on (a, b), if $x_1 < x_2 \Rightarrow f(x_1) < f(x_2)$ $\forall$ $x_1, x_2 \in (a, b)$. Thus, $f(x)$ is strictly increasing on (a, b) if the values of $f(x)$ increases with the increase in the values of x. Graphically, $f(x)$ is said to be increasing on (a, b), if the graph $y = f(x)$ moves up as x moves to the right.

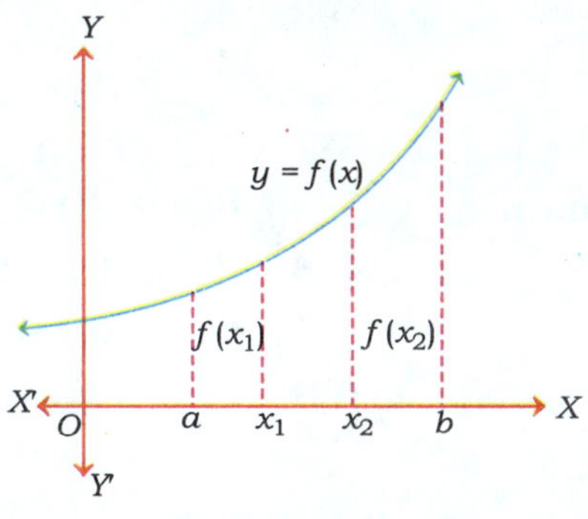

Fig. 11.2

2. Decreasing Function

A function $f(x)$ is said to be a strictly decreasing function on (a, b), if $x_1 < x_2 \Rightarrow f(x_1) > f(x_2)$ $\forall\ x_1, x_2 \in (a, b)$. Thus, $f(x)$ is strictly decreasing on (a, b), if the values of $f(x)$ decrease with increase in the values of x.

Graphically, it means that $f(x)$ is a decreasing function on (a, b), if its graph moves down as x moves to the right.

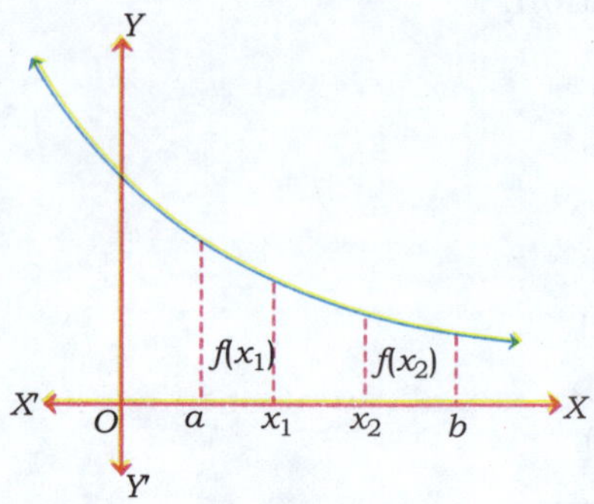

Fig. 11.3

Viva-Voce

Q.1 Write the neccessary condition for a function to be strictly increasing.

Ans A function $f(x)$ is said to be strictly increasing on (a, b), if $x_1 < x_2 \Rightarrow f(x_1) < f(x_2)\ \forall\ x_1, x_2 \in (a, b)$.

Q.2 Write the neccessary condition for a function to be strictly decreasing.

Ans A function $f(x)$ is said to be strictly decreasing on (a, b), if $x_1 < x_2 \Rightarrow f(x_1) > f(x_2)\ \forall\ x_1, x_2 \in (a, b)$

Q.3 The derivative of a function at a point is negative. State whether it is increasing or decreasing.

Ans Decreasing.

Q.4 Define monotonic function.

Ans A function $f(x)$ is said to be monotonic on an interval (a, b) if it is either increasing or decreasing on (a, b).

Q.5 State whether $f(x) = \tan x - x$ is increasing or decreasing in its domain.

Ans We have, $f(x) = \tan x - x$

$$\therefore \quad f'(x) = \sec^2 x - 1 > 0 \forall\ x \in R$$

Therefore, $f(x)$ is increasing function.

Q.6 State whether $f(x) = \sin x$ is increasing or decreasing on the interval $\left[\frac{-\pi}{2}, \frac{\pi}{2}\right]$.

Ans We have, $f(x) = \sin x$

$$\therefore \quad f'(x) = \cos x \geq 0 \forall\ x \in \left[\frac{-\pi}{2}, \frac{\pi}{2}\right]$$

Hence, $f(x)$ is increasing function.

Q.7 Can you say, whether $f(x) = x^3 - 3x^2 + 4x$ is increasing or decreasing on R?

Ans We have, $f(x) = x^3 - 3x^2 + 4x$

$$\therefore \quad f'(x) = 3x^2 - 6x + 4$$
$$= 3x^2 - 6x + 3 + 1$$
$$= 3(x^2 - 2x + 1) + 1$$
$$= 3(x - 1)^2 + 1$$

$\therefore\ f'(x) > 0\ \forall\ x \in R$.

Hence, $f(x)$ is an increasing function.

8 If $f'(x) = 0$ for each $x \in (a, b)$, then f is a constant function in $[a, b]$, true or false?

Ans True.

Activity 12

OBJECTIVE

To understand the concepts of local maxima, local minima and point of inflection.

Material Required

Drawing board, some pieces of wire, glue, white sheet.

Prerequisite Knowledge

Concept of local maxima, local minima and point of inflection.

Method of Construction

1. Take a drawing board of suitable size and paste a white sheet on it.
2. Take two pieces of wires and fix them on the sheet on the drawing board in the form of X-axis and Y-axis.
3. Take another wire of suitable length and bend it in the shape of a curve. Fix this curved wire on the white sheet pasted on the drawing board, as shown in Figure 12.1.

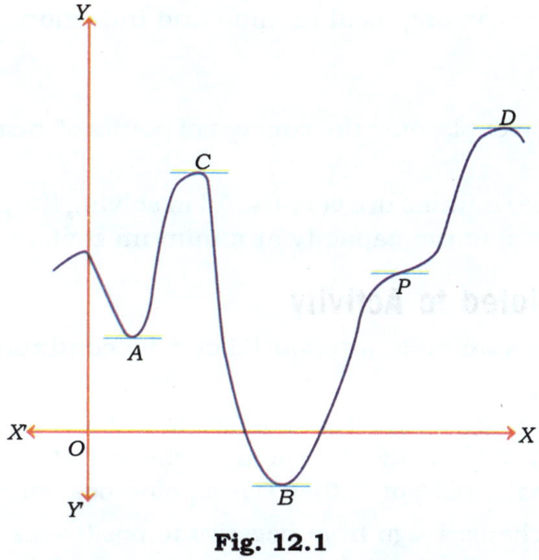

Fig. 12.1

4. Take five more wires each of length 1.5 cm (say) and fix them at the points A, C, B, P and D as shown in Figure 12.1.

Demonstration

1. In the Figure 12.1, wires at the points A, C, B, P and D represent tangents to the curve and are parallel to the axis. The slopes of tangents at these points are zero, i.e. the value of the first derivative at these points is zero. The tangent at P intersects the curve.
2. The sign of the first derivative changes from negative to positive at the points A and B. So, they are the points of local minima.

3. The sign of the first derivative changes from positive to negative at the points C and D. So, they are the points of local maxima.

4. At the point P, sign of first derivative does not change. So, it is a point of inflection.

Observations

1. Sign of the slope of the tangent (first derivative) at a point on the curve to the immediate left of A is ______.
2. Sign of the slope of the tangent (first derivative) at a point on the curve to the immediate right of A is______.
3. Sign of the first derivative at a point on the curve to immediate left of B is ______.
4. Sign of the first derivative at a point on the curve to immediate right of B is ______.
5. Sign of the first derivative at a point on the curve to immediate left of C is ______.
6. Sign of the first derivative at a point on the curve to immediate right of C is ______.
7. Sign of the first derivative at a point on the curve to immediate left of D is ______.
8. Sign of the first derivative at a point on the curve to immediate right of D is ______.
9. Sign of the first derivative at a point immediate left of P is ______ and immediate right of P is______.
10. A and B are points of local ______.
11. C and D are points of local ______.

Result

We have found point of local maxima, local minima and inflection.

Applications

1. This activity is helpful in explaining the concept of points of local maxima, local minima and inflection.
2. The concepts of maxima/minima are very useful in solving the problems of daily life such as making of packets of maximum capacity at minimum cost.

Necessary Concepts Related to Activity

Let f be a function defined on an open interval I. Let f be continuous at a critical point C in I. Then,

(i) **Local Maxima** If $f'(x)$ changes sign from positive to negative as x increases through C, i.e. if $f'(x) > 0$ at every point sufficiently close and to the left of C, and $f'(x) < 0$ at every point sufficiently close and to the right of C, then C is a point local maxima.

(ii) **Local Minima** If $f'(x)$ changes sign from negative to positive as x increases through C, i.e. if $f'(x) < 0$ at every point sufficiently close and to the left of C, and $f'(x) > 0$ at every point sufficiently close to and to the right of C, then C is point of local minima.

(iii) **Point of inflection** If $f'(x)$ does not change sign as x increases through C, then C is neither a point of local maxima nor a point of local minima. Infact, such a point is called point of inflection.

Viva-Voce

Q.1 Explain the maximum value of a function.

Ans Let $f(x)$ be a function with domain $D \subset R$. Then, $f(x)$ is said to attain the maximum value at a point $a \in D$, if $f(x) \leq f(a)$ for all $x \in D$.

Q.2 Explain the minimum value of a function.

Ans Let $f(x)$ be a function with domain $D \subset R$. Then, $f(x)$ is said to attain the minimum value at a point $a \in D$, if $f(x) \geq f(a)$ for all $x \in D$.

Q.3 How does the sign of the derivative changes at point of local minima?

Ans Sign of the derivative changes from negative to positive at point of local minima.

Q.4 How does is the sign of the derivative changes at point of local maxima?

Ans Sign of the derivative changes from positive to negative.

Q.5 What is the value of a, for which the function $f(x) = a \sin x + \left(\frac{1}{3}\right) \sin 3x$ has an extremum at $x = \pi/3$?

Ans If $f(x)$ has an extremum at $x = \pi/3$, then

$f'(x) = 0$ at $x = \pi/3$

Now, $f(x) = a \sin x + \frac{1}{3} \sin 3x$

$\Rightarrow f'(x) = a \cos x + \cos 3x$

$\therefore f'(\pi/3) = 0 \Rightarrow a \cos(\pi/3) + \cos \pi = 0 \Rightarrow a = 2$

Q.6 If $f(x) = a \log|x| + bx^2 + x$ has its extremum value at $x = -1$ and $x = 2$, then what is the value of a and b?

Ans $f(x) = a \log|x| + bx^2 + x$

$f'(x) = \frac{a}{x} + 2bx + 1$

Since, $f(x)$ attains its extremum value at $x = -1, 2$

$\therefore f'(-1) = 0$ and $f'(2) = 0$

$\Rightarrow -a - 2b + 1 = 0$ and $\frac{a}{2} + 4b + 1 = 0$

$\Rightarrow a = 2$ and $b = -1/2$

Activity 13

OBJECTIVE

To understand the concepts of absolute maximum, minimum values of a function in a given closed interval through its graph.

Material Required

Cardboard, white sheet, glue, geometry box, pencil, eraser, sketch pens, ruler, calculator, graph paper.

Prerequisite Knowledge

Concept of absolute maxima and absolute minima.

Method of Construction

1. Paste a graph paper of suitable size on a cardboard using glue.
2. Draw two perpendicular lines on the graph paper representing the two rectangular axes.
3. Graduate the two axes as shown in Figure 13.1.

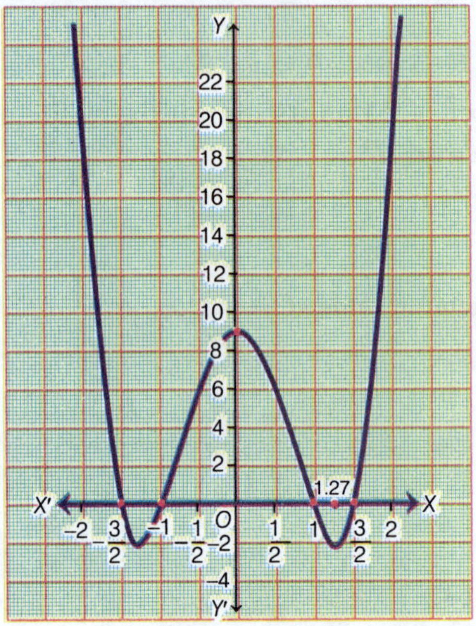

Fig. 13.1

4. Let the given function be $f(x) = (4x^2 - 9)(x^2 - 1)$ and the interval be $[-2, 2]$.
5. Taking different values of x in $[-2, 2]$, find the values of $f(x)$ and plot the ordered pairs $(x, f(x))$.
6. Obtain the graph of the function by joining the plotted points by a free hand curve as shown in the Figure 13.1.

Demonstration

1. Some ordered pairs satisfying $f(x)$ are as follows

x	0	±0.5	±1.0	±1.25	±1.27	±1.5	±2
$f(x)$	9	6	0	−1.55	−1.56	0	21

2. Plotting these points on the graph paper and joining the points by a free hand curve, the curve obtained is shown in the Figure 13.1.

Observations

1. The absolute maximum value of $f(x)$ is .... at $x =$ ....
2. Absolute minimum value of $f(x)$ is .... at $x =$ ....

Result

We have understood the concept of absolute maximum/minimum values of a function in a closed interval graphically.

Application

This activity is useful in finding the absolute maximum/minimum value of a function graphically.

Note Consider $f(x) = (4x^2 - 9)(x^2 - 1)$

$f(x) = 0$ gives the values of x as $\pm\frac{3}{2}$ and $\pm$ 1.

Both these values of x lie in the given closed interval $[-2, 2]$.

$f'(x) = (4x^2 - 9)2x + 8x(x^2 - 1) = 16x^3 - 26x = 2x(8x^2 - 13)$

$f'(x) = 0$ gives $x = 0$, $x = \pm\sqrt{\frac{13}{8}} = \pm 1.27$. These two values of x lie in $[-2, 2]$

The function has local maxima/minima at $x = 0$ and $x = \pm 1.27$.

Also, check the value of the function at the ends points of $[-2, 2]$ i.e. at $x = 2$ and $x = -2$

The function may have local maxima/minima at $x = \pm 2$.

Now,

$f(0) = 9$, $f(2) = 21$, $f(-2) = 21$, $f(1.27) = -1.56$ and $f(-1.27) = -1.56$

Hence, absolute maximum value of the function at $x = \pm 2$ is 21 and absolute minimum value of function at $x = \pm 1.27$ is -1.56.

Necessary Concepts Related to Activity

1. Absolute Maxima and Absolute Minima

Let $y = f(x)$ be a function defined on $[a, b]$. By a local maximum (or local minimum) value of a function at a point $c \in [a, b]$, we mean the greatest (or the least) value in the immediate neighbourhood of $x = c$. It does not mean the greatest or the maximum (or the least or the minimum) of $f(x)$ in the interval $[a, b]$. A function may have a number of local maxima or local minima in a given interval and even a local minimum may be greater than a local maximum.

Thus, a local maximum value may not be the greatest (the maximum) value and a local minimum value may not be the least (the minimum) value of the function in any given interval as shown in Figure 13.2.

However, if a function $f(x)$ is differentiable and continuous on a closed interval $[a, b]$, then it attains the absolute maximum (or absolute minimum) at critical points (points where $f'(x) = 0$) or at the end points of the interval $[a, b]$. Thus, to find the absolute maximum (or absolute minimum) value of the function, we choose the largest and the smallest amongst the numbers $f(a)$, $f(c_1)$, $f(c_2)$, ..., $f(c_n)$, $f(b)$ where $x = c_1, c_2, \ldots, c_n$ are the critical points.

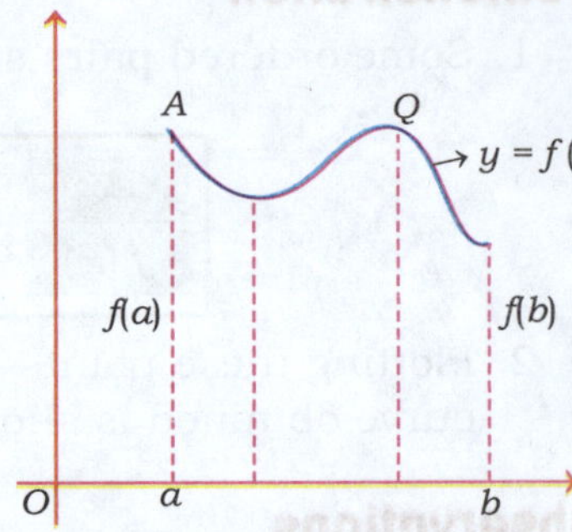

Fig. 13.2

Viva-Voce

Q.1 Write the definition of absolute maximum value of a function.

Ans Let $f(x)$ be a function with domain $D \subset R$. Then, $f(x)$ is said to attain the maximum value at a point $a \in D$, if $f(x) \le f(a)$ for all $x \in D$

Q.2 Write the definition of absolute minimum value of a function.

Ans Let $f(x)$ be a function with domain $D \subset R$. Then, $f(x)$ is said to attain the minimum value at a point $a \in D$, if $f(x) \ge f(a)$ for all $x \in D$

Q.3 Write the definition of critical point.

Ans A point c in the domain of a function f at which either $f'(c) = 0$ or f is not differentiable is called a critical point of f.

Directions (Q. Nos. 4-7) Consider the following graph of curve $f(x)$.

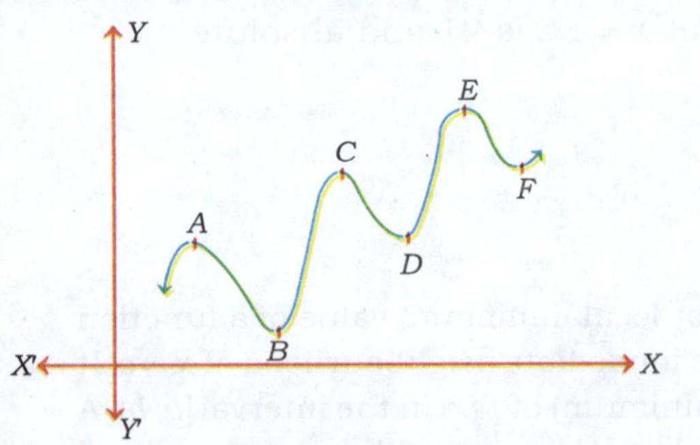

Fig. 13.2

Q.4 Identify the points of local maxima.

Ans Point of local maxima are A, C, E.

Q.5 Identify the points of local minima.

Ans Point of local minima are B, D, F.

Q.6 Identify the point of absolute maxima.

Ans Point of absolute maxima is E.

Q.7 Identify the point of absolute minima.

Ans Point of absolute minima is B.

Q.8 What is the greatest value of the function $f(x) = \sin^{-1} x^2$ in the interval $\left[\frac{-1}{\sqrt{2}}, \frac{1}{\sqrt{2}}\right]$?

Ans We have, $f(x) = \sin^{-1} x^2$

$$\Rightarrow \quad f'(x) = \frac{2x}{\sqrt{1-x^4}}$$

$$\therefore \quad f'(x) = 0$$

$$\Rightarrow \quad \frac{2x}{\sqrt{1-x^4}} = 0 \Rightarrow x = 0$$

Now, $f\left(-\frac{1}{\sqrt{2}}\right) = \sin^{-1}\left(-\frac{1}{2}\right) = -\frac{\pi}{6}$,

$f\left(\frac{1}{\sqrt{2}}\right) = \sin^{-1}\frac{1}{2} = \frac{\pi}{6}$,

and $f(0) = \sin^{-1}(0) = 0$.

Hence, the greatest value is $\frac{\pi}{6}$.

Activity 14

OBJECTIVE

To construct an open box of maximum volume from a given rectangular sheet by cutting equal squares from each corner.

Material Required

Chart papers, scissors, cellotape, calculator.

Prerequisite Knowledge

1. Concept of maxima.
2. Concept of minima.

Method of Construction

1. Take a rectangular chart paper of size 20 cm × 10 cm and name it as *ABCD*.
2. Cut four equal squares each of side x cm from each corner *A*, *B*, *C* and *D*.

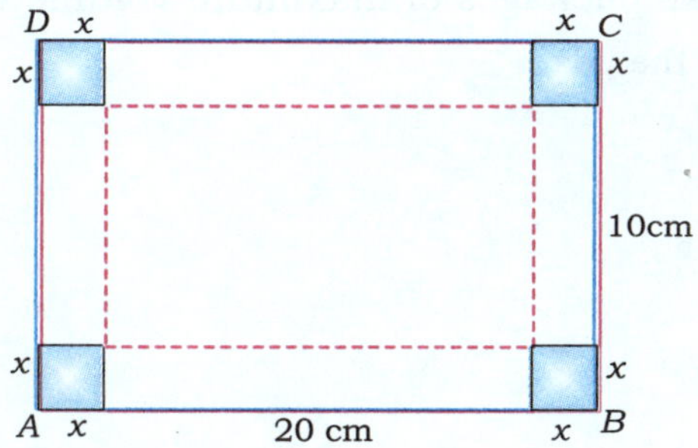

Fig. 14.1

3. Repeat the process by taking the same size of chart papers and different values of x.
4. Make an open box by folding the chart paper along each side.

Demonstration

1. When, $x = 1$, Volume of the box = 144 cm^3.
2. When $x = 1.5$, Volume of the box = 178.5 cm^3.
3. When $x = 1.8$, Volume of the box = 188.9 cm^3.
4. When $x = 2$, Volume of the box = 192 cm^3.
5. When $x = 2.1$, Volume of the box = 192.4 cm^3.
6. When $x = 2.2$, Volume of the box = 192.2 cm^3.
7. When $x = 2.5$, Volume of the box = 187.5 cm^3.
8. When $x = 3$, Volume of the box = 168 cm^3.

Clearly, volume of the box is maximum when $x = 2.1$.

Observations

1. V_1 = Volume of the open box (when $x = 1.6$) = ...
2. V_2 = Volume of the open box (when $x = 1.9$) = ...
3. V = Volume of the open box (when $x = 2.1$) = ...
4. V_3 = Volume of the open box (when $x = 2.2$) = ...
5. V_4 = Volume of the open box (when $x = 2.4$) = ...
6. V_5 = Volume of the open box (when $x = 3.2$) = ...
7. Volume V_1 is .... than volume V.
8. Volume V_2 is .... than volume V.
9. Volume V_3 is .... than volume V.
10. Volume V_4 is .... than volume V.
11. Volume V_5 is .... than volume V.

So, volume of the open box is maximum when $x =$ ....

Result

Volume of the open box is maximum, when $x = 2.1$.

Application

This activity is very useful in understanding the concepts of maxima / minima of functions. By using this concept we can make packages of maximum volume with minimum cost.

Note Let V denote the volume of the box.

Now, $V = (20 - 2x)(10 - 2x)x$

Or $V = 200x - 60x^2 + 4x^3$

$$\frac{dV}{dx} = 200 - 120x + 12x^2$$

$$\frac{dV}{dx} = 4(3x^2 - 30x + 50)$$

For maxima or minima, we have

$$\frac{dV}{dx} = 0, \text{ i.e. } 3x^2 - 30x + 50 = 0$$

i.e. $$x = \frac{30 \pm \sqrt{900 - 600}}{6} = 7.9 \text{ or } 2.1 \qquad \left[\because x = \frac{-b \pm \sqrt{b^2 - 4ac}}{2a}\right]$$

Reject $x = 7.9$

$$\frac{d^2V}{dx^2} = -120 + 24x$$

When $x = 2.1$, $\frac{d^2V}{dx^2}$ is negative.

Hence, V should be maximum at $x = 2.1$.

Necessary Concepts Related to Activity

Refer to Activity 13.

Viva-Voce

Q.1 Let f be a continuous function on an interval $I = [a, b]$. Then, f has the absolute maximum value and f attains it atleast once in I. Is it true or false?

Ans True

Q.2 Let f be a differentiable function on a closed interval I and let c be any interior point of I, then $f'(c) = 0$, if f attains its absolute maximum value at c. Is it true or false?

Ans True

Q.3 Define extreme value.

Ans A function $f(x)$ is said to have an extreme value in domain I, if there exists a point c in interval I such that $f(c)$ is either a maximum or minimum value.

Q.4 Maxima and minima do not occur alternately. Is it true or false?

Ans False

Q.5 What is the necessary condition for a point $x = c$ to be an extreme point of the function $f(x)$?

Ans $f'(c) = 0$.

Q.7 If $f(x)$ is continuous function in its domain, then how many maximum or minimum must lie between two equal values of $f(x)$?

Ans Atleast one maximum or minimum must lie between two equal values of a continuous function.

Activity 15

OBJECTIVE

To find the time when the area of a rectangle of given dimensions become maximum, if the length is decreasing and the breadth is increasing at given rates.

Material Required

Coloured sheet, paper cutter, scale, pencil, eraser, drawing board.

Prerequisite Knowledge

Concept of rate of change.

Method of Construction

1. Take a rectangle R_1 of dimensions 14 cm× 7 cm.
2. Let the length of the rectangle be decreasing at the rate of 1 cm/sec and the breadth increasing at the rate of 2 cm/sec.
3. Cut other rectangle R_2, R_3, R_4, R_5, R_6, R_7, R_8, R_9 of dimensions 13cm × 9cm, 12cm× 11cm, 11 cm× 13 cm, 10 cm× 15 cm, 9 cm× 17 cm, 8 cm× 19 cm, 7 cm× 21 cm, 6 cm× 23 cm as shown in Figure 15.1.

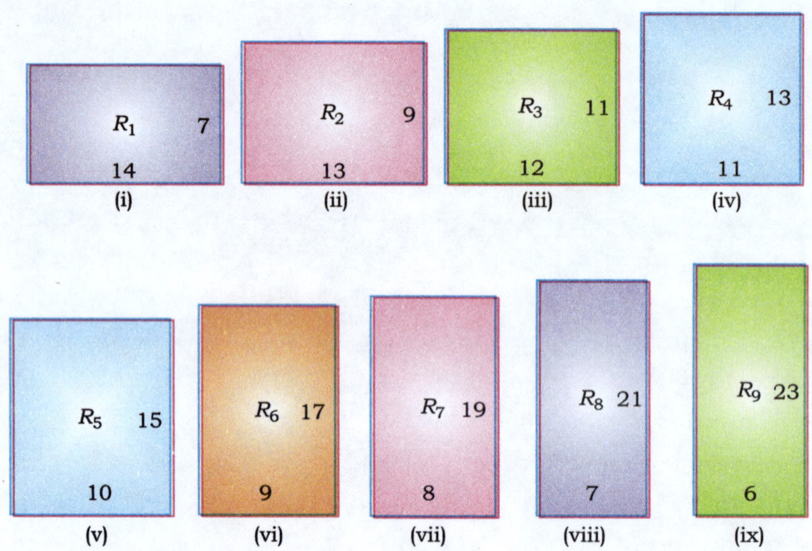

Fig. 15.1

Demonstration

1. Length of the rectangle is decreasing at the rate of 1 cm/sec and the breadth is increasing at the rate of 2 cm/sec.
2. (i) Area of the given rectangle $R_1 = 14 \times 7 = 98 \text{ cm}^2$
   (ii) Area of rectangle $R_2 = 13 \times 9 = 117 \text{ cm}^2$ (after 1 sec).
   (iii) Area of rectangle $R_3 = 12 \times 11 = 132 \text{ cm}^2$ (after 2 sec).
   (iv) Area of rectangle $R_4 = 11 \times 13 = 143 \text{ cm}^2$ (after 3 sec).
   (v) Area of rectangle $R_5 = 10 \times 15 = 150 \text{ cm}^2$ (after 4 sec).
   (vi) Area of rectangle $R_6 = 9 \times 17 = 153 \text{ cm}^2$ (after 5 sec).
   (vii) Area of rectangle $R_7 = 8 \times 19 = 152 \text{ cm}^2$ (after 6 sec).
   (viii) Area of rectangle $R_8 = 7 \times 21 = 147 \text{ cm}^2$ (after 7 sec).
   (ix) Area of rectangle $R_9 = 6 \times 23 = 138 \text{ cm}^2$ (after 8 sec) and so on.

   Thus, the area of the rectangle is maximum after 5 sec.

Observations

1. Area of the rectangle R_2 (after 1 sec) = ________.
2. Area of the rectangle R_3 (after 2 sec) = ________.
3. Area of the rectangle R_4 (after 3 sec) = ________.
4. Area of the rectangle R_5 (after 4 sec) = ________.
5. Area of the rectangle R_6 (after 5 sec) = ________.
6. Area of the rectangle R_7 (after 6 sec) = ________.
7. Area of the rectangle R_8 (after 7 sec) = ________.
8. Area of the rectangle R_9 (after 8 sec) = ________.

   Thus, area of the rectangle is maximum after ________ sec.

   And maximum area of the rectangle is ________.

Result

Area of the rectangle is maximum after 5 sec.

Application

This activity can be used in explaining the concept of rate of change and optimisation of a function.

Note Let the length and breadth of rectangle be a and b.

The length of rectangle after t sec $= a - t$.

The breadth of rectangle after t sec $= b + 2t$.

Area of the rectangle (after t sec) $= A(t) = (a - t)(b + 2t) = ab - bt + 2at - 2t^2$

$A'(t) = -b + 2a - 4t$

For maxima or minima, $A'(t) = 0$.

Putting $A'(t) = 0$, $t = \frac{2a - b}{4}$. Also, $A''(t) = -4 \Rightarrow A''\left(\frac{2a - b}{4}\right) = -4$, which is negative.

Thus, $A(t)$ is maximum at $t = \frac{2a - b}{4}$ sec. Here, $a = 14$ cm, $b = 7$ cm.

Thus, $t = \frac{28 - 7}{4} = 5.25$ s

Hence, after 5 sec, the area will become maximum.

Suggested Activity

Do same activity taking dimensions 20 cm × 10 cm of the rectangle.

Necessary Concepts Related to Activity

Rate of Change of Quantity

Let $y = f(x)$ be a function of x. Let Δy be the change in y corresponding to a small change Δx in x. Then, $\frac{\Delta y}{\Delta x}$ represents the change in y due to a unit change in x. In other words, $\frac{\Delta y}{\Delta x}$ represents the average rate of change of y with respect to x as x changes from x to $x + \Delta x$. At $\Delta x \to 0$, the limiting value of this average rate of change of y with respect to x in the interval $[x, x + \Delta x]$ becomes the instantaneous rate of change of y with respect to x.

Thus, $\lim_{\Delta x \to 0} \frac{\Delta y}{\Delta x}$ = Instantaneous rate of change of y with respect to x.

$\Rightarrow \frac{dy}{dx}$ = Rate of change of y with respect to x. $\left[\because \lim_{\Delta x \to 0} \frac{\Delta y}{\Delta x} = \frac{dy}{dx}\right]$

Hence, $\frac{dy}{dx}$ represents the rate of change of y with respect to x for a definite value of x.

Viva-Voce

Q.1 What is the significance of this activity?

Ans This activity helps us to explain the concept of rate of measure.

Q.2 Find the rate of change of area of a spherical ballon with respect to its radius.

Ans Let A and r be the area and radius of the spherical ballon, respectively. Then,

$$A = 4\pi r^2$$

$$\Rightarrow \frac{dA}{dr} = 8\pi r$$

Q.3 Explain rate of change.

Ans Suppose one quantity y varies with another quantity, say x satisfying the rule $y = f(x)$, then $\frac{dy}{dx}$ or $f'(x)$ represents the rate of change of y with respect to x.

Q.4 If a rectangle has constant perimeter, then find the rate of change of perimeter.

Ans $P = C$ (where C is constant)

$$\Rightarrow \frac{dP}{dt} = 0.$$

Q.5 Find an angle θ, where $0 < \theta < \frac{\pi}{2}$, which increases twice as fast as its sine.

Ans We have, $\frac{d\theta}{dt} = 2\frac{d}{dt}(\sin\theta)$

$$\Rightarrow \frac{d\theta}{dt} = 2\cos\theta\frac{d\theta}{dt}$$

$$\Rightarrow \cos\theta = \frac{1}{2} \Rightarrow \theta = \frac{\pi}{3}$$

Q.6 Define rate of change mathematically.

Ans If $y = f(x)$, then

$$\lim_{x \to 0} \frac{\Delta y}{\Delta x} = \frac{dy}{dx}$$

Q.7 Find the surface area of a sphere when its volume is increasing at the same rate as its radius is increasing.

Ans Given, $\frac{dV}{dt} = \frac{dr}{dt}$

$$\frac{d}{dt}\left(\frac{4}{3}\pi r^3\right) = \frac{dr}{dt} \Rightarrow 4\pi r^2\frac{dr}{dt} = \frac{dr}{dt}$$

$$\Rightarrow r = \frac{1}{2\sqrt{\pi}}$$

$$\therefore S = 4\pi r^2 = 1 \text{ sq unit}$$

Activity 16

OBJECTIVE

To verify that amongst all the rectangles of the same perimeter, the square has the maximum area.

Material Required

Drawing sheet, paper/sheet cutter, scale, pencil, eraser, drawing board, gum etc.

Prerequisite Knowledge

1. Concept of maxima
2. Concept of minima

Method of Construction

1. Take a drawing board of a suitable size and fix a white sheet on it.
2. Make rectangles each of perimeter say 52 cm on a drawing sheet. Rectangles of different dimensions are as follows

   R_1 : 18 cm × 8 cm, R_2 : 17 cm × 9 cm, R_3 : 16 cm × 10 cm, R_4 : 15 cm × 11 cm, R_5 : 14 cm × 12 cm, R_6 : 13 cm × 13 cm, R_7 : 12.5 cm × 13.5 cm

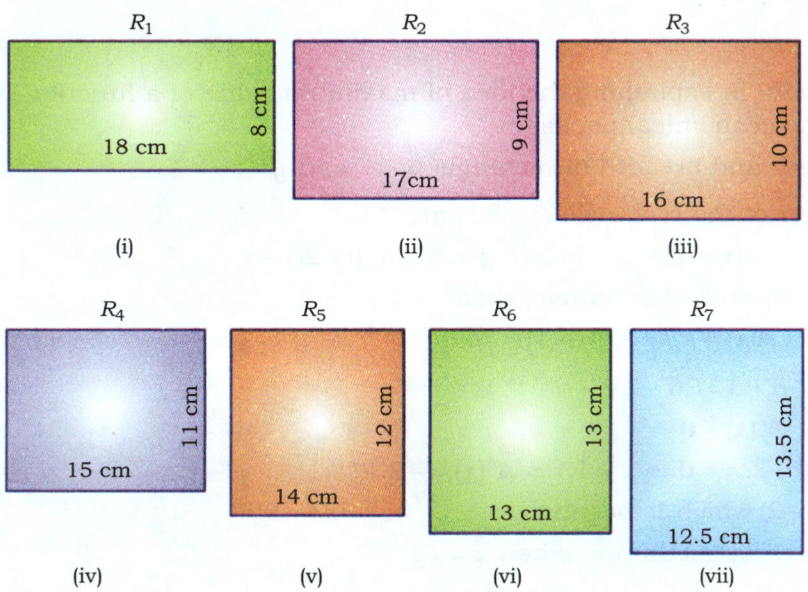

Fig. 16.1

3. Cut out these rectangles and paste them on the white sheet on the drawing board (see Figure 16.1(i) to (vii)).

Demonstration

1. Area of rectangle $R_1 = 18 \text{ cm} \times 8\text{cm} = 144\text{cm}^2$

   Area of rectangle $R_2 = 17 \text{ cm} \times 9 \text{ cm} = 153 \text{ cm}^2$

   Area of $R_3 = 160\text{cm}^2$

   Area of $R_4 = 165\text{cm}^2$

   Area of $R_5 = 168\text{cm}^2$

   Area of $R_6 = 169\text{cm}^2$

   Area of $R_7 = 168.75\text{cm}^2$

2. Perimeter of each rectangle is same but their areas are different. Area of rectangle R_6 is the maximum, which is a square of side 13 cm. This can also be verified using theoretical description given in the note.

Observations

1. Perimeter of each rectangle R_1, R_2, R_3, R_4, R_5, R_6, R_7 is ....
2. Area of the rectangle R_4 .... than the area of rectangle R_6.
3. Area of the rectangle R_7 .... than the area of rectangle R_6.
4. The rectangle R_6 has the dimensions .... × .... and hence it is a ....
5. Of all the rectangles with same perimeter, the .... has the maximum area.

Result

Amongst all rectangles with the same perimeter, the square has the maximum area.

Application

This activity is useful in explaining the idea of maximum value of a function. The result is also useful in preparing economical packages.

Note Let the length and breadth of rectangle be x and y.

The perimeter of the rectangle $P = 52$ cm.

$$2(x + y) = 52 \text{ or } x + y = 26 \text{ or } y = 26 - x$$

Let $A(x)$ be the area of rectangle, then

$$A(x) = xy = x(26 - x) = 26x - x^2$$

$\Rightarrow$ $A'(x) = 26 - 2x$

Now, $A'(x) = 0$

$\Rightarrow$ $26 - 2x = 0 \Rightarrow x = 13 \Rightarrow A''(x) = -2$

$A''(x = 13) = -2$, which is negative

Therefore, area is maximum, when $x = 13$

$$y = 26 - 13 = 13 = x$$

So, $x = y = 13$

Hence, amongst all rectangles, the square has the maximum area.

Necessary Concepts Related to Activity

Refer to Activity 13.

Viva-Voce

Q.1 How do you check if a function $f(x)$ has the maximum value at its critical point?

Ans If the sign of $f''(x)$ is negative, function has the maximum value.

Q.2 How do you check if a function $f(x)$ has the minimum value at its critical point?

Ans If the sign of $f''(x)$ is positive, function has the minimum value.

Q.3 Write the condition for finding critical points of a function $f(x)$.

Ans For critical points put $f'(x) = 0$.

Q.4 Area of a rectangle can be maximised by taking all its sides equal. Is it true or false?

Ans True

Q.5 Write one real life application of this activity.

Ans This activity can be used in minimising the amount of material required to make a container and maximising its area.

**Q.6 Area of a right angle triangle of given hypotenuse is maximum, when triangle is isosceles.
Is it true or false?**

Ans True

Activity 17

OBJECTIVE

To verify geometrically that $\vec{c} \times (\vec{a} + \vec{b}) = \vec{c} \times \vec{a} + \vec{c} \times \vec{b}$

Material Required

Geometry box, cardboard, white paper, cutter, sketch pen, cellotape.

Prerequisite Knowledge

Concept of cross-product.

Method of Construction

1. Fix a white paper on the cardboard of suitable size.
2. Draw a line segment OA (= 8 cm, say) and let it represents $\vec{c}$.
3. Draw another line segment OB (= 6 cm, say) at an angle (say 60°) with OA.

   Let $\overrightarrow{OB} = \vec{a}$

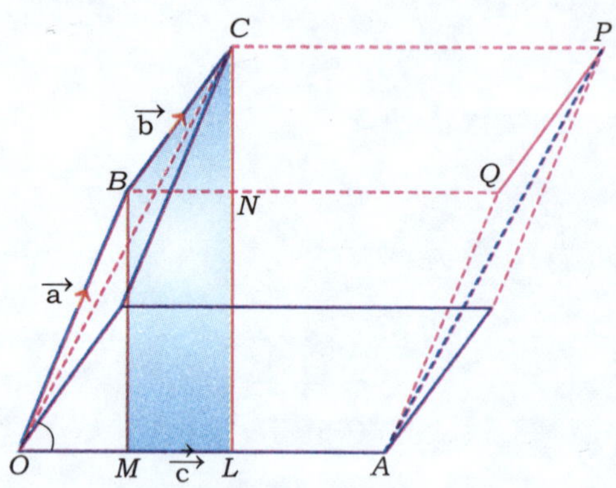

Fig. 17.1

4. Draw BC (= 5 cm, say) making an angle (say 30°) with $\overrightarrow{OA}$. Let $\overrightarrow{BC} = \vec{b}$
5. Draw perpendiculars BM, CL and BN.
6. Complete parallelograms $OAPC$, $OAQB$ and $BQPC$.

Demonstration

1. $\overrightarrow{OC} = \overrightarrow{OB} + \overrightarrow{BC} = \vec{a} + \vec{b}$
2. Let $\angle COA = \alpha$
3. We know that $|\vec{c} \times (\vec{a} + \vec{b})| = |\vec{c}|\,|\vec{a} + \vec{b}|\sin\alpha$ = Area of parallelogram *OAPC*.
4. Again, $|\vec{c} \times \vec{a}|$ = Area of parallelogram *OAQB*.
5. Also, $|\vec{c} \times \vec{b}|$ = Area of parallelogram *BQPC*.
6. Therefore, Area of parallelogram *OAPC* = $(OA)(CL)$

$$= (OA)\,(LN + NC) = (OA)\,(BM + NC) = (OA)(BM) + (OA)(NC)$$

= Area of parallelogram *OAQB* + Area of parallelogram *BQPC*

$$= |\vec{c} \times \vec{a}| + |\vec{c} \times \vec{b}|$$

So, $\quad |\vec{c} \times (\vec{a} + \vec{b})| = |\vec{c} \times \vec{a}| + |\vec{c} \times \vec{b}|$

Direction of each of these vectors, $\vec{c} \times (\vec{a} + \vec{b})$, $\vec{c} \times \vec{a}$ and $\vec{c} \times \vec{b}$ is perpendicular to the same plane.

So, $\vec{c} \times (\vec{a} + \vec{b}) = \vec{c} \times \vec{a} + \vec{c} \times \vec{b}$

Observation

$|\vec{c}| = |\overrightarrow{OA}| = OA =$ ______

$|\vec{a} + \vec{b}| = |\overrightarrow{OC}| = OC =$ ______

$CL =$ ______

$|\vec{c} \times (\vec{a} + \vec{b})|$ = Area of parallelogram *OAPC* = $(OA)(CL)$ = ________ sq units ...(i)

$|\vec{c} \times \vec{a}|$ = Area of parallelogram *OAQB* = $(OA)(BM)$ = ______ × ______ = ______ ...(ii)

$|\vec{c} \times \vec{b}|$ = Area of parallelogram *BQPC* = $(OA)(CN)$ = ______ × ______ = ______ ...(iii)

From Eqs. (i), (ii) and (iii), we get

Area of parallelogram *OAPC* = Area of parallelogram *OAQB* + Area of parallelogram ______

Thus, $|\vec{c} \times (\vec{a} + \vec{b})| = |\vec{c} \times \vec{a}| + |\vec{c} \times \vec{b}|$

$\vec{c} \times \vec{a}$, $\vec{c} \times \vec{b}$ and $\vec{c} \times (\vec{a} + \vec{b})$ are all in the direction of ______ to the plane of paper.

Therefore, $\vec{c} \times (\vec{a} + \vec{b}) = \vec{c} \times \vec{a} +$ ______

Result We have verified that $\vec{c} \times (\vec{a} + \vec{b}) = \vec{c} \times \vec{a} + \vec{c} \times \vec{b}$.

Application

This activity is also helpful in explaining the distributive property of vector multiplication over addition. This activity can also be performed by taking rectangles instead of parallelograms.

Note This activity can also be performed by taking rectangles instead of parallelograms.

Necessary Concepts Related to Activity

Vector (or Cross) Product

Let $\vec{a}$, $\vec{b}$ be two non-zero non-parallel vectors. Then, the vector product $\vec{a} \times \vec{b}$, in that order is defined as a vector whose magnitude is $|\vec{a}||\vec{b}|\sin\theta$, where θ is the angle between $\vec{a}$ and $\vec{b}$ and whose direction is perpendicular to the plane of $\vec{a}$ and $\vec{b}$ in such a way that $\vec{a}$, $\vec{b}$ and this direction constitute a right handed system.

In other words, $$\vec{a} \times \vec{b} = |\vec{a}||\vec{b}|\sin\theta\hat{n}$$

where θ is the angle between $\vec{a}$ and $\vec{b}$, and $\hat{n}$ is a unit vector perpendicular to the plane of $\vec{a}$ and $\vec{b}$ such that $\vec{a}$, $\vec{b}$, $\hat{n}$ form a right handed system.

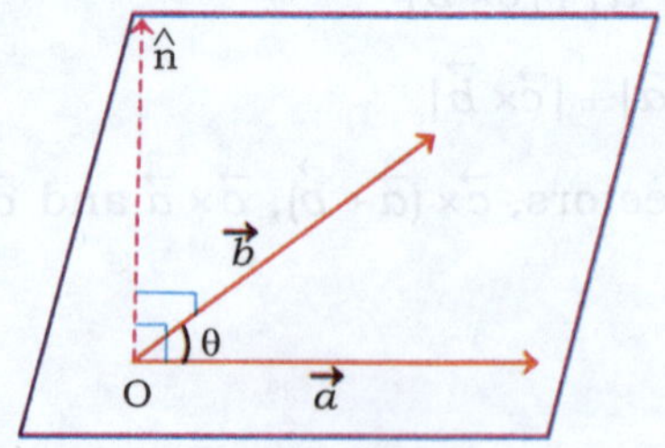

Fig. 17.2

When we say that $\vec{a}$, $\vec{b}$, $\hat{n}$ form a right handed system it means that, if we rotate vector $\vec{a}$ into the vector $\vec{b}$, then $\hat{n}$ will point in the direction perpendicular to the plane of $\vec{a}$ and $\vec{b}$ in which a right handed screw will move if it is turned in the same manner.

Viva-Voce

Q.1 Given for any two vectors $\vec{a}$ and $\vec{b}$, is $\vec{a} \times \vec{b} = \vec{b} \times \vec{a}$? Is the cross-product of vectors commutative?

Ans As, $\vec{a} \times \vec{b} \neq \vec{b} \times \vec{a}$, cross-product of vectors is not commutative.

Q.2 Write the formula for vector product of two vectors.

Ans $\vec{a} \times \vec{b} = |\vec{a}||\vec{b}|\sin\theta\hat{n}$

Q.3 Whether the vector product of two vectors is vector or scalar.

Ans The vector product of two vectors is always a vector.

Q.4 If $\vec{a} \times \vec{b} = \vec{0}$, what can be concluded about the vectors $\vec{a}$ and $\vec{b}$?

Ans It can be concluded that both the vectors are parallel or collinear to each other.

Q.5 Write the formula for the area of a parallelogram with adjacent sides $\vec{a}$ and $\vec{b}$.

Ans Area of a parallelogram whose adjacent sides are $\vec{a}$ and $\vec{b} = |\vec{a} \times \vec{b}|$.

Q.6 If for any three vectors, we have $\vec{a} \times \vec{b} = \vec{c}$, then what is relation between them?

Ans $\vec{c}$ will be perpendicular to both $\vec{a}$ and $\vec{b}$ i.e. $\vec{a} \perp \vec{c}$ and $\vec{b} \perp \vec{c}$.

Q.7 Write a unit vector which is perpendicular to both $\vec{a}$ and $\vec{b}$.

Ans Let $\hat{c}$ is required vector.

Then, $\hat{c} = \pm \dfrac{\vec{a} \times \vec{b}}{|\vec{a} \times \vec{b}|}$

Activity 18

OBJECTIVE

To verify that angle in a semi-circle is a right angle, using vector method.

Material Required

Drawing board, white sheet, glue, pens, geometry box, eraser, wires, paper arrow heads.

Prerequisite Knowledge

1. Concept of dot product of two vectors.
2. Concept of equal vectors.

Method of Construction

1. Take a thick drawing board of size 25 cm× 25 cm.
2. On the drawing board, paste a white sheet of the same size using glue.
3. On this sheet, draw a circle, with centre *O* and radius 10 cm (say).

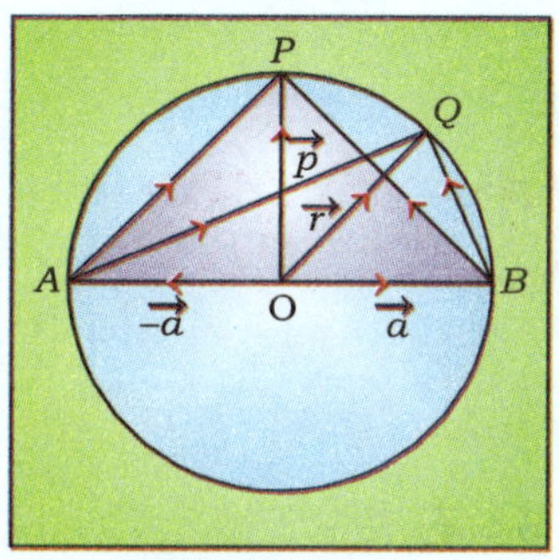

Fig. 18.1

4. Fix pins at the points *O, A, B, P* and *Q*. Join *OP, OA, OB, AP, AQ, BQ, OQ* and *BP* using wires.
5. Put arrows on *OA, OB, OP, AP, BP, OQ, AQ* and *BQ* to show them as vectors, using paper arrow heads, as shown in the Figure 18.1.

Demonstration

By actual measurement

1. Using a protractor, measure the angle between the vectors $\overrightarrow{AP}$ and $\overrightarrow{BP}$, $\angle APB = 90°$.
2. Similarly, the angle between the vectors $\overrightarrow{AQ}$ and $\overrightarrow{BQ}$ is $\angle AQB = 90°$.
3. Repeat the above process by taking some more points *R, S, T*, ... on the semi-circles, forming vectors *AR, BR; AS, BS; AT, BT*; ..., etc., i.e. angle formed between two vectors in a semi-circle is a right angle.

Observation

By vector method,

$|\overrightarrow{OP}| = |\overrightarrow{OA}| = |\overrightarrow{OB}| = |\overrightarrow{OQ}| = r = a = p =$ ______

$|\overrightarrow{AP}| =$ ______, $|\overrightarrow{BP}| =$ ______, $|\overrightarrow{AB}| =$ ______

$|\overrightarrow{AQ}| =$ ______, $|\overrightarrow{BQ}| =$ ______

$|\overrightarrow{AP}|^2 + |\overrightarrow{BP}|^2 =$ ______, $|\overrightarrow{AQ}|^2 + |\overrightarrow{BQ}|^2 =$ ______

So, $\angle APB =$ ______ and $\overrightarrow{AP} \cdot \overrightarrow{BP}$ ______ $\angle AQB =$ ______ and $\overrightarrow{AQ} \cdot \overrightarrow{BP} =$ ______

Similarly, for points R, S, T, ______

$\angle ARB =$ ______, $\angle ASB =$ ______, $\angle ATB =$ ______ , ______

i.e. angle in a semi-circle is a right angle.

Result

We have proved that angle in a semi-circle is a right angle.

Application

This activity can be used to explain the concepts of

(i) opposite vectors

(ii) vectors of equal magnitude

(iii) perpendicular vectors

(iv) dot product of two vectors.

Note Let $OA = OB = a = OP = p$

$\overrightarrow{OA} = -\vec{a}$, $\overrightarrow{OB} = \vec{a}$, $\overrightarrow{OP} = \vec{p}$

$\overrightarrow{AP} = -\overrightarrow{OA} + \overrightarrow{OP} = \vec{a} + \vec{p}$, $\overrightarrow{BP} = \vec{p} - \vec{a}$.

$\overrightarrow{AP} \cdot \overrightarrow{BP} = (\vec{p} + \vec{a}) \cdot (\vec{p} - \vec{a}) = |\vec{p}|^2 - |\vec{a}|^2 = 0$ $\qquad [\because |\vec{p}| = |\vec{a}|]$

So, the $\angle APB$ between the vectors $\overrightarrow{AP}$ and $\overrightarrow{BP}$ is a right angle.

Similarly, $\overrightarrow{AQ} \cdot \overrightarrow{BQ} = 0$, so $\angle AQB = 90^\circ$ and so on.

Necessary Concepts Related to Activity

1. The Scalar or Dot Product

Let $\vec{a}$ and $\vec{b}$ be two non-zero vectors inclined at an angle θ. Then, the scalar product of $\vec{a}$ and $\vec{b}$ is denoted by $\vec{a} \cdot \vec{b}$ and is defined as $\vec{a} \cdot \vec{b} = |\vec{a}||\vec{b}|\cos\theta$.

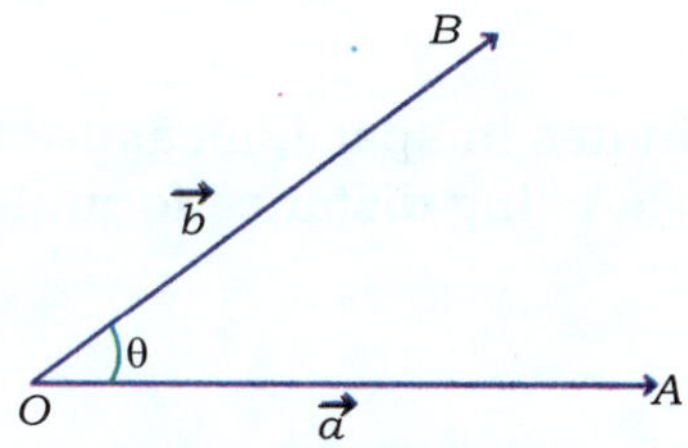

Fig. 18.2

Clearly, the scalar product of two vectors is a scalar quantity, due to which this product is called scalar product. Since, we are putting a dot between $\vec{a}$ and $\vec{b}$, therefore it is also called dot product.

2. Equal Vectors

Two vectors are said to be equal, if they have same magnitude and direction regardless of the positions of their initial points. Symbolically if $\vec{a}$ and $\vec{b}$ are equal, then it is written as $\vec{a} = \vec{b}$

Viva-Voce

Q.1 Write the dot products of two vectors.

Ans If $\vec{a}$ and $\vec{b}$ are two non-zero vectors inclined at an angle θ, then

$$\vec{a} \cdot \vec{b} = |\vec{a}||\vec{b}|\cos\theta$$

Q.2 The dot product of two vectors is a scalar quantity. Is it true or false?

Ans True

Q.3 If $\vec{a}$, $\vec{b}$ are two non-zero vectors and $\vec{a} \cdot \vec{b} = 0$, what can be said about $\vec{a}$ and $\vec{b}$?

Ans It can be concluded that both $\vec{a}$ and $\vec{b}$ are perpendicular to each other.

Q.4 Is $\vec{a} \cdot \vec{b} = \vec{b} \cdot \vec{a}$ i.e. the scalar product of two vectors commutative?

Ans Yes, the scalar product of two vectors follows commutativity.

Q.5 Angle in a semi-circle is a right angle. Is it true or false?

Ans True

Q.6 If $\vec{a}$ and $\vec{b}$ are unit vectors such that $\vec{a} \cdot \vec{b} = \cos\theta$, then find the value of $|\vec{a} + \vec{b}|$.

Ans We have, $|\vec{a} + \vec{b}|^2 = |\vec{a}|^2 + |\vec{b}|^2 + 2(\vec{a} \cdot \vec{b})$

$$\Rightarrow \quad |\vec{a} + \vec{b}|^2 = 1 + 1 + 2\cos\theta = (2 + 2\cos\theta) = 2(1 + \cos\theta) = 4\cos^2\frac{\theta}{2} \quad \left[\because 1 + \cos\theta = 2\cos^2\frac{\theta}{2}\right]$$

$$\Rightarrow \quad |\vec{a} + \vec{b}| = 2\cos\frac{\theta}{2}$$

Activity 19

OBJECTIVE

To locate the points to given coordinates in space, measure the distance between two points in space and then to verify the distance using distance formula.

Material Required

Cardboard, geometry box, graph paper, pins of different lengths, paper arrows.

Prerequisite Knowledge

1. Concept of 3-Dimensional geometry.
2. Coordinates of a point in space.
3. Concept of distance formula.

Method of Construction

1. Take a cardboard and paste a graph paper on it.
2. Draw two lines $X'OX$ and $Y'OY$ to represent X-axis and Y-axis, respectively as shown in Figure 19.1 and take 1 unit = 1 cm.

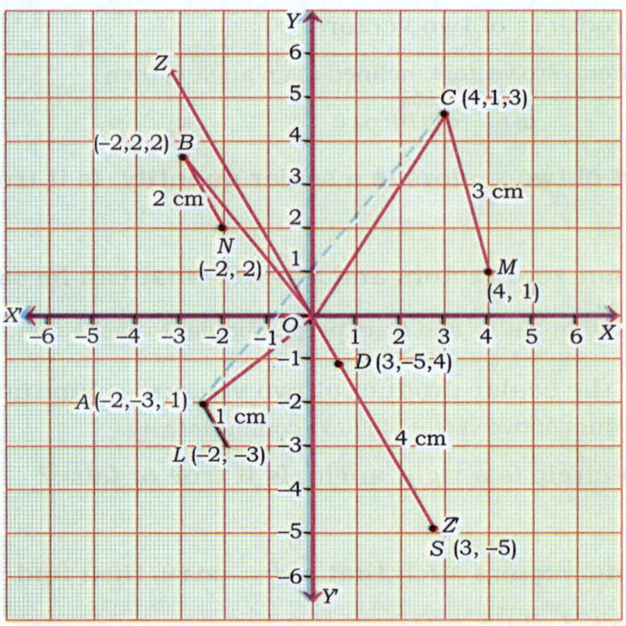

Fig. 19.1

3. Fix a wire through O, in the vertical direction, representing the Z-axis.
4. Fix pins of length 1 cm, 2 cm, 3 cm, 4 cm, etc. at different points on the graph paper (say at $L(-2, -3)$, $N(-2, 2)$, $M(4, 1)$, $S(3, -5)$, etc.

   Now, the upper tips of these pins represent the points (say A, B, C, D) in the space.

Demonstration

1. Coordinates of the point $A = (-2, -3, 1)$.
2. Coordinates of the point $B = (-2, 2, 2)$.
3. Similarly, find the coordinates of the points C and D.
4. By actual measurement (using a scale) distance $AB = 5.1$ cm
5. By distance formula, $AB = \sqrt{(-2+2)^2 + (-3-2)^2 + (1-2)^2} = \sqrt{26} = 5.099$

   Thus, the distance AB, obtained by actual measurement is approximately same as the distance obtained by using the distance formula.

   Same can be verified for other pairs of points $A, C; B, C; A, D; C, D; B, D$.

Observation

Coordinates of the point C = ...

Coordinates of the point D = ...

On actual measurement :

AC = ..., BC = ...

AD = ..., CD = ...,

BD = ...

Using distance formula AC = ...,

BC = ..., AD = ...

CD = ..., BD = ...

Result

The distance between two points in space obtained on actual measurement and by using distance formula is approximately the same.

Application

1. This activity is useful in visualising the position of different points in space (coordinates of points).
2. The concept of position vectors can also be explained through this activity.

Necessary Concepts Related to Activity

1. Three Dimensional Geometry

Let XOX', YOY' and ZOZ' be three mutually perpendicular lines intersecting at O, where the point O is the **origin** and the lines $X'OX$, $Y'OY$ and $Z'OZ$ are called X-axis, Y-axis and Z-axis, respectively. These three lines are also called the **rectangular coordinates axes** and together constitute the rectangular coordinate system.

The axes X, Y and Z, when takes in pairs determine three mutually perpendicular planes XOY, YOZ and ZOX or simply XY-plane, YZ-plane and ZX-plane called the **rectangular coordinate planes**, which further divide the space into eight parts called **octants**.

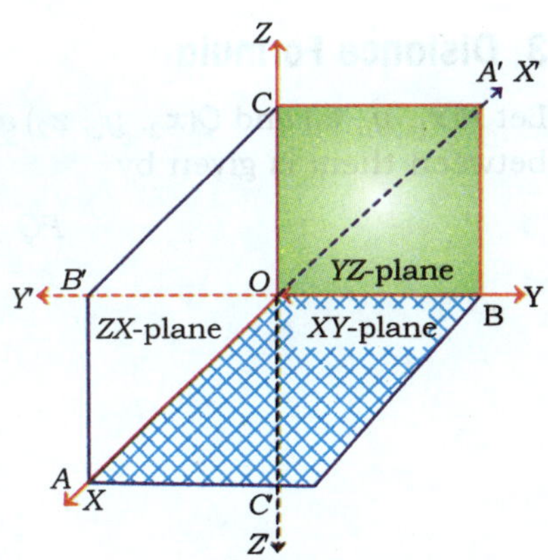

Fig. 19.2

2. Coordinates of a Point in Space

The coordinates of a point are the distances from the origin to the feet of the perpendiculars, drawn from the point on the respective coordinates axes.

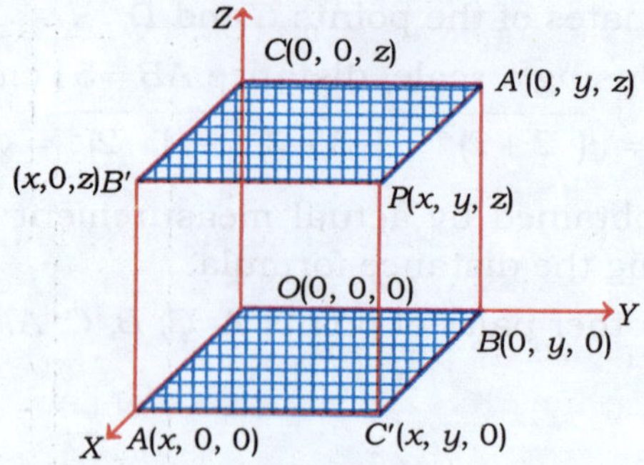

Fig. 19.3

The coordinates of any point on the X-axis, Y-axis and Z-axis will be as $A(x, 0, 0)$, $B(0, y, 0)$ and $C(0, 0, z)$, respectively.

The coordinates of any point of XY, YZ and ZX-planes may be taken as $(x, y, 0)$, $(0, y, z)$ and $(x, 0, z)$, respectively.

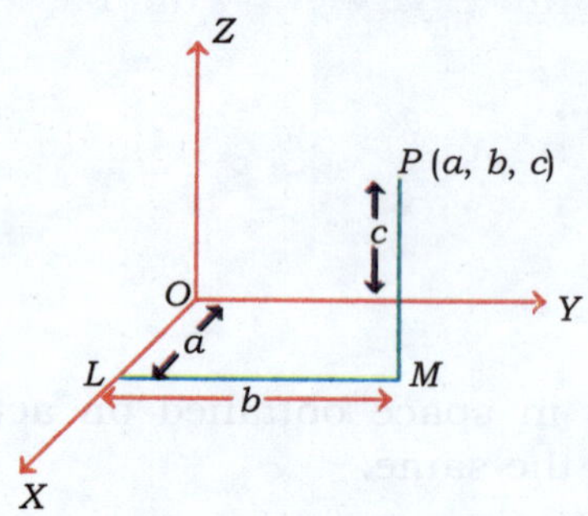

Fig. 19.4

If we are given the coordinates (a, b, c) of a point P and we have to locate the point, then first fix the point L on X-axis such that $OL = a$. Now, find a point M on the perpendicular to X-axis at point L such that $LM = b$. We can say that M has coordinates (a, b) in XY-plane. Having reached the point M, we draw the perpendicular on XY-plane at point M and locate a point P on this perpendicular such that $PM = c$. The point P so obtained has the coordinates (a, b, c).

3. Distance Formula

Let $P(x_1, y_1, z_1)$ and $Q(x_2, y_2, z_2)$ are two points referred to a system of rectangular axes, then distance between them is given by

$$PQ = \sqrt{(x_2 - x_1)^2 + (y_2 - y_1)^2 + (z_2 - z_1)^2}$$

Viva-Voce

Q.1 Write the distance formula between two points $P(x_1, y_1, z_1)$ and $Q(x_2, y_2, z_2)$.

Ans The distance between two points $P(x_1, y_1, z_1)$ and $Q(x_2, y_2, z_2)$ is given by

$$PQ = \sqrt{(x_2 - x_1)^2 + (y_2 - y_1)^2 + (z_2 - z_1)^2}$$

Q.2 Define coordinates of a point.

Ans The coordinates of a point are the distances from the origin to the feet of perpendicular drawn from the point on the respective coordinate axes.

Q.3 Define rectangular coordinate system.

Ans If $X'OX$, $Y'OY$ and $Z'OZ$ are three mutually perpendicular lines intersecting at the origin, then these lines are called the rectangular coordinate axes, which together constitute the rectangular coordinate system.

Q.4 Define rectangular coordinate plane.

Ans The three axes X, Y, Z, when taken in pairs form three mutually perpendicular planes namely XY, YZ and ZX called the rectangular coordinate plane.

Q.5 What is the locus of a point (x, y, z) for which $x = 0$, $y = 0$?

Ans Z-axis.

Q.6 Write the coordinates of the foot of perpendicular from the point (1, 2, 3) on X-axis.

Ans We know that y and z-coordinates of any point lie on X-axis are zero, therefore coordinates of the foot of perpendicular from the point (1, 2, 3) on X-axis are (1, 0, 0).

Q.7 Find the distance between the points $P(-1, 2, 3)$ and $Q(2, 0, -3)$.

Ans $PQ = \sqrt{[(2 - (-1))]^2 + [0 - 2]^2 + [-3 - 3]^2}$

$\Rightarrow PQ = \sqrt{(3)^2 + (-2)^2 + (-6)^2}$

$\Rightarrow PQ = \sqrt{9 + 4 + 36} = \sqrt{49} = 7$ units

Activity 20

OBJECTIVE

To measure the shortest distance between two skew-lines and verify it analytically.

Material Required

A piece of cardboard of size 40 cm × 30 cm, graph paper, three wooden block of size 2 cm × 2 cm × 2 cm each and one wooden blocks of size 2 cm × 2 cm × 4 cm, some wires of different lengths, set squares, gum, pen/pencil, etc.

Prerequisite Knowledge

1. Concept of skew-lines.
2. Concept of distance between two skew-lines.

Method of Construction

1. Paste a graph paper on a piece of cardboard.
2. On the graph paper, draw two lines *OA* and *OB* to represent *X*-axis and *Y*-axis, respectively.

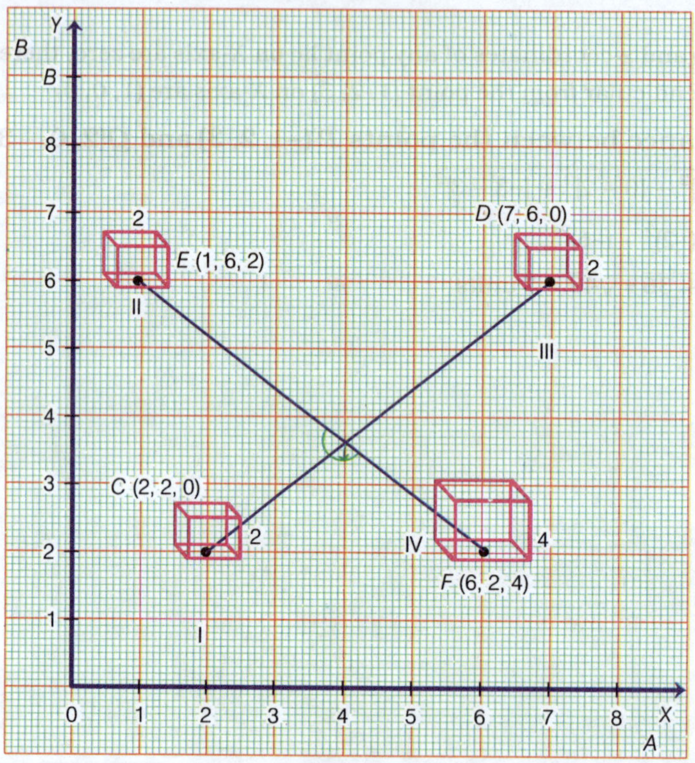

Fig. 20.1

3. Name the three blocks of size 2 cm × 2 cm × 2 cm as I, II and III. Name the other wooden block of size 2 cm × 2 cm × 4 cm as IV.
4. Place blocks I, II, III such that their base centres are at the points (2, 2), (1, 6) and (7, 6), respectively, and block IV with its base centre at (6, 2).

5. Place a wire joining the points C and D, the centres of the tops of the blocks I and III and another wire joining the centres E and F of the bases of blocks II and IV as shown in Figure 20.1.
6. The lines represented by these two wires are skew-lines.
7. Take a wire and join it perpendicularly with the skew-lines and calculate the actual distance.

Demonstration

1. A set-square is placed in such a way that its one perpendicular side is along the wire CD.
2. Move the set-square along CD till its other perpendicular side touches the other wire.
3. Using set-squares, measure the distance between the two lines in this position. This is known as the shortest distance between two skew-lines.
4. Analytically, find the equation of line joining $C(2, 2, 0)$ and $D(7, 6, 0)$ and other line joining $E(1, 6, 2)$ and $F(6, 2, 4)$ and find SD using $\left|\frac{(\vec{a}_2 - \vec{a}_1).(\vec{b}_1 \times \vec{b}_2)}{|\vec{b}_1 \times \vec{b}_2|}\right|$. The two distances obtained will be equal.

Observations

1. Coordinates of point C are ....
2. Coordinates of point D are ....
3. Coordinates of point E are ....
4. Coordinates of point F are ....
5. Equation of line CD is ....
6. Equation of line EF is ....

Shortest distance between CD and EF analytically = ...

Shortest distance by actual measurement = ...

The results so obtained are ....

Result

We have measured the shortest distance between two skew-lines.

Application

This activity can be used to explain the concept of skew-lines and the shortest distance between two skew-lines in space.

Necessary Concepts Related to Activity

1. Skew Lines

If two lines are neither intersecting nor-parallel, then such pair of lines are non-coplanar and are called skew-lines.

2. Shortest Distance between Two Skew-Lines

For skew-lines, the line of the shortest distance will be perpendicular to both the lines and it is unique also. In Figure 20.2, the shortest distance (SD) between two skew-lines L_1 and L_2 is the length of the line segment PQ .

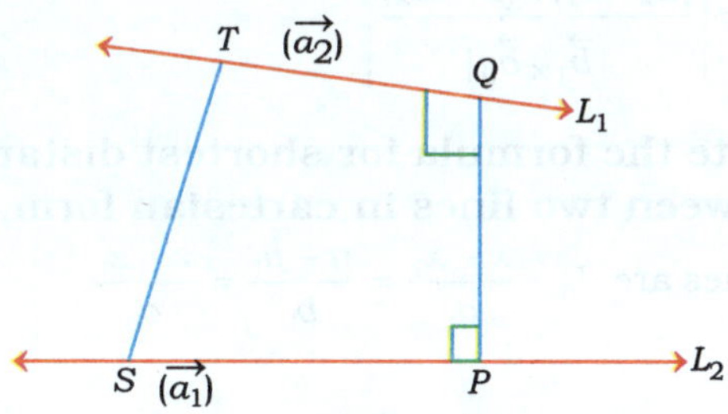

Fig. 20.2

Vector Form

Let L_1 and L_2 be two skew-lines with equations $\vec{r} = \vec{a}_1 + \lambda \vec{b}_1$ and $\vec{r} = \vec{a}_2 + \mu \vec{b}_2$

Then, shortest distance PQ between these two skew-lines is

$$SD = \left|\frac{(\vec{a_2}-\vec{a_1})\cdot(\vec{b_1}\times\vec{b_2})}{|\vec{b_1}\times\vec{b_2}|}\right|$$

Cartesian Form

Let L_1 and L_2 be two skew-lines with equations

$$L_1: \frac{x-x_1}{a_1} = \frac{y-y_1}{b_1} = \frac{z-z_1}{c_1} \text{ and } L_2: \frac{x-x_2}{a_2} = \frac{y-y_2}{b_2} = \frac{z-z_2}{c_2}$$

Then, the shortest distance between these lines is

$$\left|\frac{\begin{vmatrix} x_2-x_1 & y_2-y_1 & z_2-z_1 \\ a_1 & b_1 & c_1 \\ a_2 & b_2 & c_2 \end{vmatrix}}{\sqrt{(b_1c_2-b_2c_1)^2+(c_1a_2-c_2a_1)^2+(a_1b_2-a_2b_1)^2}}\right|$$

Viva-Voce

Q.1 Define skew-lines.

Ans Two straight lines in space which are neither parallel nor intersecting are called skew-lines.

Q.2 Explain line of shortest distance between two skew-lines.

Ans If l_1 and l_2 are two skew-lines, then there is one and only one line perpendicular to each of lines l_1 and l_2 which is known as the line of shortest distance.

Q.3 Write the formula for shortest distance between two lines in vector form.

Ans If lines are $L_1 : \vec{r} = \vec{a_1} + \lambda \vec{b_1}$

and $L_2 : \vec{r} = \vec{a_2} + \mu \vec{b_2}$, then

$$SD = \left|\frac{(\vec{a_2}-\vec{a_1})\times(\vec{b_1}\times\vec{b_2})}{|\vec{b_1}\times\vec{b_2}|}\right|$$

Q.4 Write the formula for shortest distance between two lines in cartesian form.

Ans If lines are $L_1 : \frac{x-x_1}{a_1} = \frac{y-y_1}{b_1} = \frac{z-z_1}{c_1}$

and $L_2 : \frac{x-x_2}{a_2} = \frac{y-y_2}{b_2} = \frac{z-z_2}{c_2}$, then

$$SD = \left|\frac{\begin{vmatrix} x_2-x_1 & y_2-y_1 & z_2-z_1 \\ a_1 & b_1 & c_1 \\ a_2 & b_2 & c_2 \end{vmatrix}}{\sqrt{(b_1c_2-b_2c_1)^2+(c_1a_2-c_2a_1)^2+(a_1b_2-a_2b_1)^2}}\right|$$

Q.5 Skew-lines do not lie in the same plane. Is it true or false?

Ans True

Q.6 Write the condition for two given lines to intersect.

Ans If the lines $\vec{r} = \vec{a_1} + \lambda \vec{b_1}$

and $\vec{r} = \vec{a_2} + \mu \vec{b_2}$

intersect, then the shortest distance between them is zero.

$$\therefore \left|\frac{(\vec{b_1}\times\vec{b_2})\cdot(\vec{a_2}-\vec{a_1})}{|\vec{b_1}\times\vec{b_2}|}\right| = 0 \Rightarrow (\vec{b_1}\times\vec{b_2})\cdot(\vec{a_2}-\vec{a_1}) = 0$$

Activity 21

OBJECTIVE

To explain the computation of conditional probability of a given event A, when event B has already occurred, through an example of throwing a pair of dice.

Material Required

A piece of cardboard, white sheet, pencil, scale, a pair of dice, glue etc.

Prerequisite Knowledge

1. Concept of sample space.
2. Concept of conditional probability.

Method of Construction

1. Fix a white sheet on a piece of cardboard of a suitable size.
2. Make a square and divide it into 36 unit squares of size 1.5 cm (say) each (see Figure 21.1)
3. Write the pair of numbers as shown in the Figure 21.1.

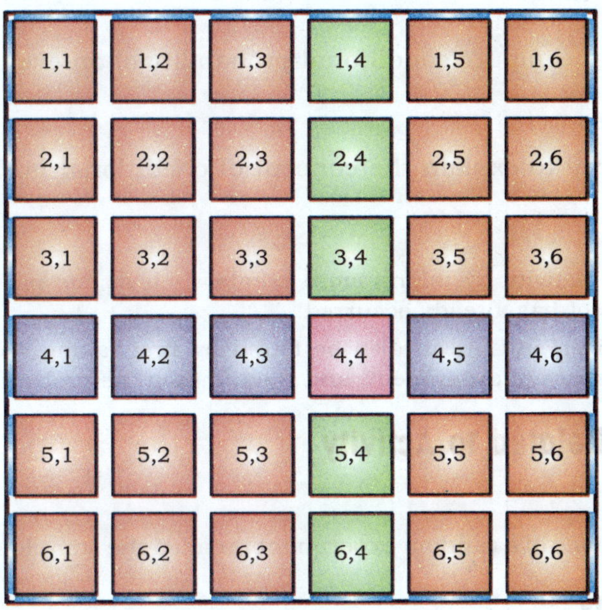

Fig. 21.1

Demonstration

1. Figure 21.1 gives all possible outcomes of the given experiment. Hence, it gives the sample space of the experiment.
2. Suppose we have to find the conditional probability of an event A if an event B has already occurred, where A is the event "a number 4 appears on both the dice" and B is the event "4 has appeared on at least one of the dice" i.e. we have to find $P(A / B)$.
3. From Figure 21.1 number of outcomes favourable to $A = 1$

   Number of outcomes favourable to $B = 11$

   Number of outcomes favourable to $A \cap B = 1$.
4. (i) $P(A) = \frac{1}{36}$ (ii) $P(B) = \frac{11}{36}$,

   (iii) $P(A \cap B) = \frac{1}{36}$ (iv) $P(A / B) = \frac{P(A \cap B)}{P(B)} = \frac{1}{11}$

Observations

1. Outcomes favourable to A : ...., $n(A)$ = ...
2. Outcomes favourable to B : ...., $n(B)$ = ...
3. Outcomes favourable to $A \cap B$: ......, $n(A \cap B)$ = ...
4. $P(A \cap B)$ = ...
5. $P(A / B)$ = ... = ...

Result

We have explained how to compute conditional probability of an event.

Application

This activity is very helpful to explain the concept of conditional probability, which is further used in Bayes' theorem.

Note

(i) You may repeat this activity by taking more events such as the probability of getting a sum 10 when a doublet has already occurred.

(ii) Conditional probability $P(A / B)$ can also be found by first taking the sample space of event B out of the sample space of experiment, and then finding the probability A from it.

Necessary Concepts Related to Activity

1. Sample Space

The set of all possible outcomes of a random experiment is called the sample space associated with it.

2. Conditional Probability

Let A and B be two events associated with a random experiment. Then, the probability of occurrence of event A under the condition that B has already occurred and $P(B) \neq 0$, is called the conditional probability and it is denoted by $P(A / B)$.

$$P\left(\frac{A}{B}\right) = \frac{P(A \cap B)}{P(B)}$$

Thus, we have $P(A / B)$ = Probability of occurrence of A given that B has already occurred.

Similarly, $P(B / A)$ where $P(A) \neq 0$ is defined as the probability of occurrence of event B when A has already occurred.

$$P\left(\frac{B}{A}\right) = \frac{P(B \cap A)}{P(A)}$$

The meaning of symbol $P(A / B)$ and $P(B / A)$ depends on the nature of the events A and B, and also on the nature of the random experiment. These two symbols have the following meaning also.

$P(A / B)$ = Probability of occurrence of A when B has occurred

or

Probability of occurrence of A when B is taken as the sample space.

or

Probability of occurrence of A with respect to B.

and $P(B / A)$ = Probability of occurrence of B when A occurred

or

Probability of occurrence of B when A is taken as sample space.

or

Probability of occurrence of B with respect to A.

Viva-Voce

Q.1 Write the definition of an event.

Ans A subset of the sample space associated with a random experiment is called an event.

Q.2 Explain conditional probability.

Ans If A and B are two events associated with a random experiment, then the probability of occurrence of event A, given B has already occurred and $P(B) \neq 0$, is called conditional probability.

Q.3 Write the formula for finding conditional probability of an event.

Ans $P\left(\frac{A}{B}\right) = \frac{P(A \cap B)}{P(B)}$, where $P(B) \neq 0$.

Q.4 Define a random experiment.

Ans A random experiment is an experiment, trial or observation that can be repeated numerous times under the same conditions. Its outcome is independent and is fairly distributed and cannot be predicted with certainty.

Q.5 If $P(A) = \frac{2}{7}$, $P(B) = \frac{4}{7}$ and $P(A \cap B) = \frac{3}{7}$, then $P\left(\frac{A}{B}\right) = ?$

Ans $P\left(\frac{A}{B}\right) = \frac{P(A \cap B)}{P(B)} = \frac{\frac{3}{7}}{\frac{4}{7}} = \frac{3}{4}$

Q.6 Write the condition for event A and B to be independent events.

Ans Events A and B are said to be independent if $P(A \cap B) = P(A) \cdot P(B)$.

Q.7 Write one application of conditional probability.

Ans Conditional probability is used in Baye's theorem to find reverse probability of an event.

Projects

Project 1

OBJECTIVE

To minimise the cost of the food, meeting the dietary requirements of the staple food of the adolescent students of your school.

Task to be Done

(i) Make a survey of atleast 200 students for finding the staple food, which they consume on daily basis.

(ii) Select two food items, say one cereal and one pulse.

(iii) To ask the dietician person and find the minimum requirement of protein and carbohydrate for an adolescent and also find the content of protein and carbohydrate in 1 kg of selected cereal and pulse respectively.

(iv) Find the minimum cost of the selected cereal and pulse from market.

(v) Formulate the corresponding Linear Programming problem.

(vi) Draw the graph of obtained equations.

(vii) Using corner point method, solve the problem.

(viii) Calculate the result.

Project 2

OBJECTIVE

Estimation of the population of a particular region/country under the assumptions that there is no migration in or out of the existing population in a particular year.

Task to be Done

(i) Find the population of a selected region for a particular year.

(ii) Find the number of births and number of deaths in the existing population in that particular year t (say).

Suppose

$f(t)$: denote the population in a particular year t.

$B(t)$: denote the number of births in one year between t and $t+1$.

$D(t)$: denote the number of deaths in one year between t and $t+1$.

(iii) We get the relation of the form

$$f(t+1) = f(t) + B(t) - D(t) \quad \text{...(i)}$$

(iv) Now, we consider $b = \dfrac{B(t)}{f(t)}$,

which represents the birth rate for the time interval t to $t+1$.

and $d = \dfrac{D(t)}{f(t)}$,

which represents death rate for the time interval t to $t+1$.

(v) From Eq. (i), we get

$$f(t+1) = f(t) + B(t) - D(t) = f(t)\left[1 + \frac{B(t)}{f(t)} - \frac{D(t)}{f(t)}\right] = f(t)(1+b-d)$$

$$\Rightarrow \quad f(t+1) = f(t)(1+b-d) \quad \text{...(ii)}$$

(vi) Put $t = 0$ in Eq. (ii), we get

$$f(1) = f(0)(1+b-d)$$

Now, put $t = 1$ in Eq. (ii), we get

$$f(2) = f(1)(1+b-d)$$

$$f(2) = f(0)(1+b-d)^2 \quad [\because f(1) = f(0)(1+b-d)]$$

Continuing this process, we get

$$f(t) = f(0)(1+b-d)^t \quad \text{...(iii)}$$

Here, we assumed that birth rate and death rate remains the same for consecutive years. $f(0)$ denote the initial population.

Thus, Eq. (iii) gives the mathematical formula for calculating the population in t yr.

(vii) By using calculator, we can find the population in different number of years.

(viii) Compare the population data obtained theoretically and draw the inferences.

Project 3

OBJECTIVE

Finding the coordinates of different points identified in your classroom using the concepts of three dimensional geometry and also find the distances between the identified points.

Task to be Done

(i) Select any corner of your classroom as the origin.

(ii) Take three perpendicular edges of walls as coordinate system say X, Y and Z-axes.

(iii) Find the coordinates of each corner of the room, corners of windows, doors and blackboard in the classroom, etc.

(iv) Find the coordinate of each point in the space of the classroom such as tips of ceiling fan, bulbs etc.

(v) Find the distances between different points either by measurement or by using distance formula.

(vi) Find the coordinates of the diagonals of the room and length of the diagonals by distance formula.

Activity No. ____________ Date ________ Page No. ________

Teacher Signature ________________

Activity No. ____________ Date _________ Page No. _________

Teacher Signature ________________

Activity No.__________ Date ________ Page No. ________

Teacher Signature______________

Activity No. ________ Date ________ Page No. ________

Teacher Signature ____________

Activity No. ____________ Date ________ Page No. ________

Teacher Signature ________________

Activity No. ____________ Date ________ Page No. ________

Teacher Signature ________________

Activity No. ____________ Date ________ Page No. ________

Teacher Signature ________________

Activity No. ____________ Date ________ Page No. ________

Teacher Signature ____________

Activity No. ________ Date ______ Page No. ______

Teacher Signature ____________

Activity No.__________ Date ________ Page No. ________

Teacher Signature____________

Activity No. ____________ Date ________ Page No. ________

Teacher Signature ________________

Activity No. ___________ Date ________ Page No. ________

Teacher Signature ______________

Activity No. ____________ Date __________ Page No. __________

Teacher Signature ________________

Activity No. ________ Date ________ Page No. ________

Teacher Signature ________

Activity No. ________ Date ________ Page No. ________

Teacher Signature ____________

Activity No. __________ Date ________ Page No. ________

Teacher Signature ______________

Activity No. ____________ Date ________ Page No. ________

Teacher Signature ________________

Activity No. ____________ Date ________ Page No. ________

Teacher Signature ________________

Activity No. ____________ Date ________ Page No. ________

Teacher Signature ________________

Activity No. ____________ Date ________ Page No. ________

Teacher Signature ________________

Activity No.________ Date ______ Page No. ______

Teacher Signature ____________

Activity No. ___________ Date ________ Page No. ________

Teacher Signature ________________

Activity No. ____________ Date ________ Page No. ________

Teacher Signature ________________

Activity No. ____________ Date ________ Page No. ________

Teacher Signature ______________

Activity No. ________ Date ________ Page No. ________

Teacher Signature ________

Activity No. ___________ Date ________ Page No. ________

Teacher Signature ________________

Activity No. ____________ Date ________ Page No. ________

Teacher Signature ________________

Activity No. ___________ Date ________ Page No. ________

Teacher Signature ________________

Activity No. ____________ Date ________ Page No. ________

Teacher Signature ________________

Activity No. ___________ Date ________ Page No. ________

Teacher Signature ________________

Activity No. ___________ Date ________ Page No. ________

Teacher Signature ________________

Activity No. ____________ Date ________ Page No. ________

Teacher Signature ________________

Activity No. ____________ Date ________ Page No. ________

Teacher Signature ________________

Activity No. ___________ Date ________ Page No. ________

Teacher Signature ________________

Activity No. ____________ Date ________ Page No. ________

Teacher Signature ________________

Activity No. ____________ Date ________ Page No. ________

Teacher Signature________________

Activity No. ____________ Date ________ Page No. ________

Teacher Signature ________________

Activity No. ___________ Date ________ Page No. ________

Teacher Signature ________________

Activity No. ___________ Date ________ Page No. ________

Teacher Signature ______________

Activity No. ____________ Date ________ Page No. ________

Teacher Signature ________________

Activity No. ____________ Date ________ Page No. ________

Teacher Signature ________________

Activity No. ____________ Date ________ Page No. ________

Teacher Signature ________________

Activity No. ____________ Date ________ Page No. ________

Teacher Signature ________________

Activity No.__________ Date ________ Page No. ________

Teacher Signature ______________

Activity No.__________ Date ________ Page No. ________

Teacher Signature ____________

Activity No. ____________ Date ________ Page No. ________

Teacher Signature ____________

Activity No.________ Date ______ Page No. ______

Teacher Signature ____________

Activity No. ____________ Date ________ Page No. ________

Teacher Signature ________________

Activity No. ____________ Date ________ Page No. ________

Teacher Signature ________________

Activity No. ____________ Date ________ Page No. ________

Teacher Signature ________________

Activity No. ____________ Date ________ Page No. ________

Teacher Signature ________________

Activity No. ___________ Date ________ Page No. ________

Teacher Signature ________________

Activity No.___________ Date ________ Page No. ________

Teacher Signature_______________

Activity No.__________ Date ________ Page No. ________

Teacher Signature ______________

Activity No. __________ Date ________ Page No. ________

Teacher Signature ______________

Activity No. ____________ Date ________ Page No. ________

Teacher Signature ________________

Activity No. ____________ Date ________ Page No. ________

Teacher Signature ________________

Activity No. ___________ Date ________ Page No. ________

Teacher Signature ______________

Activity No. ___________ Date ________ Page No. ________

Teacher Signature ________________

Activity No.___________ Date ________ Page No. ________

Teacher Signature_______________

Activity No. ____________ Date ________ Page No. ________

Teacher Signature ________________

Activity No. ____________ Date ________ Page No. ________

Teacher Signature ________________

Activity No.___________ Date ________ Page No. ________

Teacher Signature ________________